*To Tony*

KC FOONG

# A SIMPLE GUIDE
# TO PERSONAL
# HAPPINESS

*With love,*

*March 12, 2010*

Order this book online at www.trafford.com/07-1241
or email orders@trafford.com

Most Trafford titles are also available at major online book retailers.

Note for Librarians: A cataloguing record for this book is available from Library
and Archives Canada at www.collectionscanada.ca/amicus/index-e.html

Printed in Victoria, BC, Canada.

ISBN: 978-1-4251-3300-9

*We at Trafford believe that it is the responsibility of us all, as both individuals and corporations,
to make choices that are environmentally and socially sound. You, in turn, are supporting this
responsible conduct each time you purchase a Trafford book, or make use of our publishing services.
To find out how you are helping, please visit www.trafford.com/responsiblepublishing.html*

*Our mission is to efficiently provide the world's finest, most comprehensive book publishing
service, enabling every author to experience success. To find out how to publish your book, your
way, and have it available worldwide, visit us online at www.trafford.com/10510*

 www.trafford.com

**North America & international**
toll-free: 1 888 232 4444 (USA & Canada)
phone: 250 383 6864 ♦ fax: 250 383 6804 ♦ email: info@trafford.com

**The United Kingdom & Europe**
phone: +44 (0)1865 722 113 ♦ local rate: 0845 230 9601
facsimile: +44 (0)1865 722 868 ♦ email: info.uk@trafford.com

10 9 8 7 6 5 4 3 2

## Acknowledgement

The stories shared in this book are about real people. Great care has been taken to protect the actual identities of the people, who are my best friends and the real inspiration for this book.

This book would not have been written without the values instilled in me by my father and mother. Though my father is no longer with me in the traditional sense, I feel his presence and hear his words. The wisdom, joy, and simple everyday living with happiness resonate in my mind everyday.

I want to thank my mother, Madame Koey Kek Hoon, and my late father, Mr. Foong Fock Kim (1933–2003) who have given me a life full of childhood happiness.

*My Parents,*
*Madam Koey Kek Hoon & Mr. Foong Fock Kim*

# Table of Contents

# Preface

The 240 hours that I've spent doing research, compiling information, dreaming, thinking, and writing this book for the past 60 days have made me a very happy man. In the quietness of the night, I focus on my thoughts and allow my heart speak out. Writing has become my lifelong passion. It is like meeting a good old friend on the face of each page.

May the sharing of this book inspire you, help you find the happiness you so deserve and reconnect you to your first love and the whole meaning of this life for you and you alone.

Please enjoy the journey.

KC Foong
Vancouver
British Columbia, Canada

# Introduction

This simple book reveals my personal journey from my childhood days up to now in search of happiness mostly at the right places. Section I talks about the 10 simple secrets of happiness, which you can apply in your life.

In the world today, despite being far better off financially than previous generations, we are no happier. The pursuit of happiness drives much of what we do, but achieving it always seems just out of reach. Why is it so hard to be happy? What would make you happier?

Happy people tend to engage in activities that are challenging and absorbing. Such activities help people to focus their full attention on the present moment. People who do volunteer work tend to be happier, perhaps because of "downward comparison" with others who are less fortunate. Section II further reveals the secrets of self discovery. Knowing who we are, understanding our needs and wants would allow us to set our priorities, pinpoint our strengths and discover our destinies.

Success is related to happiness–but as a consequence, not a cause, of mood. The mostly likely explanation is that happy people have other personality traits that facilitate success. Also, a positive mood is liable to result in greater motivation, as well as cooperation from others. Knowing ourselves through self discovery will open up new doors, new opportunities, and new horizons into our lives.

Section III continues the search for happiness in many unlikely situations. The roots of happiness are many, understanding the many ways that our minds work, does afford us the chance to make better choices about how we will invest our efforts and time in the pursuit of happiness.

To me, happiness is not an ultimate destination but instead lies in appreciation of the journey. I want to invite you to join me in this wonderful journey of joy, to truly know who you are and to train yourself how to be happy always.

Read this book one short chapter at a time. It is a 30 day life makeover plan which could change your entire life and destiny!

*"I didn't want to get to the end of my life*
*and find that I've just lived the length of it.*
*I want to have lived the width of it as well."*
DIANE ACKERMAN, AUTHOR

*"If you want to be happy,*
*put your effort into controlling the sail,*
*not the wind."*
ATTRIBUTION UNKNOWN

As you will see, I use one, two, or more quotations to end each chapter, providing inspiration and reflection. My hope is that these quotations, some of them by very famous people, will open up your capacity for imagination and wonder, and perhaps help you to gain access to your personal happiness!

SECTION I

# 10 SECRETS OF HAPPINESS

1

## Follow Your Passion

All through my life, I've seen people struggle. Some struggle to wake up in the morning, some struggle to sleep well at night. Some struggle to make ends meet, some struggle on what to do with their extra money. Most struggle to want to do what they want, but yet dare not follow their passions. Fear of failure, rejection, and loneliness. To follow your passion, you must believe in yourself. Think about what makes you feel most like yourself. It lives in the moments where you are most at ease in your own skin, the moments when you feel right and whatever you are doing seems like an extension of your mind, body and spirit. That's passion. Whether it is cooking noodles for a group of friends, toasting your best friend at his wedding, or mixing watercolors for your latest masterpiece. Passions are big or small, quiet or dynamic. Some people use their work to feed their passion, while others use their career to free themselves for other pursuits. Just how much you need to experience passion, fulfillment, and a sense of contribution on the job is entirely up to you.

The world will not stop revolving if you do not get to work today. The pressure of going to work is tremendous for some of us. Identify your life. Where do you want to be on 1 year's time, 3 years' time, 5 years' time, and eventually 10 years' time. Do not postpone your happiness. We may not live till tomorrow! Discover and determine what are the most important inspirations and joy to you. Is it your spouse, children, cars, work, hobbies, friends, or your image? (Not necessarily in this particular order). Once you identify what makes you the happiest, go for it.

Po Bronson in his book "What Should I Do with My Life?" said: "All this obsession about our careers. It is not what you do that's important, it's who you are. If people stopped worrying about what they do, they'd be a lot happier. Just go get a job. Enjoy your nights and weekends." Bronson provides an amazing description of what it means to contribute: "It seems that just about any profession can be performed with a confidence that it's contributing to the well-being of others—just as any profession can feel soulless and selfish. There is no official list of honorable, noble careers. The proof is in the individual's experience. You either find the pleasure of connecting with others in your daily reality or you don't—this nobility is not something that can be assigned or predetermined. Often it defies stereotypes."

During my childhood days, I discovered and experienced the joy of traveling with my parents. As busy as they were, they would bring my two sisters and me to the park where I would be bicycling or running as fast as I could in the field. I felt total freedom and the sense of belonging to the family was extraordinarily strong. When I was growing up as a teenager in Ayer Tawar, a small village in Malaysia, I often went hunting on a bicycle with five good friends using stones, rubber bands, and Y shaped sticks found in the rubber estates. We cycled deep into the jungle looking for rare birds or any other small mammals. I don't remember killing any endangered species but we definitely caught a few types of birds and mammals, skinned them, barbequed and shared the edible parts among us. Those years were my best memories of my life. Several years later, my family moved to Sitiawan, another small town in Malaysia where I indulged in bicycling into the villages, mountain tops, beaches and far away places just to watch that particular sunset day after day with a borrowed old bicycle, covering sometimes 30 miles a day! My father was too poor to afford a proper mountain bicycle but I found joy even as young as a 16 year old boy and nothing could stop me even until now.

*"Being a singer is a natural gift.*
*It means I'm using*
*to the highest degree possible*
*the gift that God gave me to use. I*
*'m happy with that."*
ARETHA FRANKLIN

*"Life is short, and it is here to be lived."*
KATE WINSLET

2

## Live Authentically

Create a new vision and find your balance. Each new year, millions of people around the world make plans to earn more money, to lose weight, to be more successful, to be more beautiful, to buy a bigger house, bigger car, to have more children and to raise more intelligent kids. This list goes on and on…usually by the third month of the exciting year, most of the wish lists are forgotten. People become tired, stick to their old routines and hope to achieve their plans somehow. Does it sound familiar? It does not take any effort for dust to settle on top of furniture. That is the law of gravity. Dust settles and the longer we ignore it, dust will likely settle even more on more furniture. To get rid of dust is easy. A gentle wipe with a damp cloth will effectively remove dust right away. To create a new vision for a new year and find our balance in life, we must commit to change and lift our heads up. Once we start to lift our heads up to evaluate our values and beliefs, we start to LIVE AUTHENTICALLY.

I have a very good friend who worked for a company for almost 25 years. He used his best mind, energy, talent, and youth to climb the corporate ladder steadily. He worked hard to raise his family. Indeed, he was a great man and a great senior manager in the established company for which he worked, until he fell sick one day. He was so sick that he did not turn up for work for three weeks. At 43, he was bedridden and fell into a coma after a minor surgery on his back. He was always telling me that he wanted to operate a small restaurant after his early retirement at 45, so that he could spend more time with his family and earn more money. Now he can't even spend time thinking about his retirement. He is deep asleep in a world somewhere. His company easily found a replacement, terminated his contract and moved on within three weeks. My heart is aching when I write this. I have gone fishing with him twice. He has always liked fishing but could never find time. I can only pray that he wakes up soon to enjoy his family before it is too late!

Yes! Before it is too late, let us all wake up and evaluate our values and beliefs. To create a new vision and find our balance, we must commit to change our lifestyle and start to live authentically. This is the second secret to finding happiness on earth. Authentic living is not about scaling mountain peaks or winning races. It's about acknowledging and developing strength of our bodies so that we can continue to live our lives as fully as possible. Create a list of things you wish you didn't spend so much time, energy, or money on. Make another list of the things you wish you could have, do, or be. Then think of ways to reconcile the two and create your authentic life, one that will bring you joy and happiness.

Listen to your heart and make choices. Every new step we take, each new opportunity that we dare to seize, repays us with a more exciting life and increased confidence in our very being. What happens when you stand up for yourself and live boldly? You begin to realize that your dreams are possible. You find a new sense of purpose. You become buoyant and alive. We all have special inclinations and individual ideas. When we come to a point, finally, where we don't brush these away as nonsense, we give ourselves the chance to find out what truly makes us happy. It begins with a desire to reverse a bad situation. They develop when we follow these intimations of happiness and dare to explore who we ourselves truly are. Take a step beyond the familiar. Who knows where a painting class might lead, or what taking up social dancing will do for your happiness, and goals, or training for a bike race, or simply deciding to read a book every month in a different subject area. It does not take an inordinate amount of energy to live creatively and happily. All we need to redesign our lives is to move toward those values that we have come to see as the most meaningful and life sustaining. What we seek, seeks us. We reignite feelings of intensity and passion that have been lying dormant for too long. We also begin to notice we are having fun too!

*"I always wanted to be someone,
but I should have been more specific."*
LILY TOMLIN, ACTRESS, COMEDIAN

*"Life is what happens
while you're busy making other plans."*
JOHN LENNON, THE BEATLES

3

## Simplify Daily Living

Celebrate today. Go reward yourself. Kiss your spouse, hug your kids, smile and shout "Good morning" to the first five people you meet every morning, let the person behind you in a queue go first in the bank, post office, or toll plaza. How many times do we get so upset when someone cuts into the line especially the spot just in front of us? If we could have known that the person was rushing back to hit the toilet, we would have gladly let him go first. Stretch your mind, and make up stories, think positively and we will not feel so bad after all. Anyway, what is five minutes if we have seventy or eighty years to live?

The best ways to simplify our daily living are to connect with nature and to nourish our souls. In the past 25 years I have traveled to about 30 countries on my own and with my family members or close friends. During all those happy trips to all four continents, I have never joined any tour groups. When I travel, my intention is to see how people live, eat, and go through their everyday life. I find total relaxation when I walk the streets like a local, buy food at a local grocery store and walk to the parks, mountains or tracks to stay fit.

When I was in New York during my early working days, I spent at least one hour every morning walking in the snow, rain or sunny day. I just love the smell of morning freshness, especially after a snow storm. The wet look on the tree trunks inspires me, the tiny rain drops from the leaves when the wind blows excites my senses and the lovely nature, the ponds, the lakes, the sound of the breeze, the laughter of children and the singing of the birds keep me walking and going.

When I visited Zurich, Switzerland, I hiked from mountain top to mountain top, admiring the trees, flowers, and the snow. The locals hike with their dogs, the senior citizens walk with their walking sticks, and the not so young run up the slopes just to glide down with their gliders. Upon landing, they would run up again to the mountain top to glide down again and again. No wonder Switzerland has the most healthy people in the world with the median age being 85! They connect with nature regularly and they are expert in nourishing their souls too, seeking pleasure in life, music, arts and food.

What makes Vancouver in British Columbia, Canada, the most livable place in the world? You are right. The Government's plans and the people's interest in connecting with nature. There are hundreds of parks, big and small, in every city in the province. Anytime of the day, I see people running, jogging, practicing "Tai-Chi" or just hanging around in the many parks the city provides. I hardly observe any overweight individual. Most people look younger than their biological age. This has to do not only with the weather, food, or culture here, but definitely with their ability to CELEBRATE TODAY, stretch their minds, think positively, connect with nature and nourish their souls. This is the third secret to finding simple but pure happiness in your life.

Simplicity means focusing on what's vital in your life. How do you decide what truly matters to you? How can you decide which luxuries you value and which you can do without? Finding the answers isn't always easy. Here are some suggestions to get you started.

### Identify what gives you energy

You shouldn't try to figure out what's essential using logic. Forget about what you think you "should" do or have. Instead, ask yourself whether something gives you energy or drains your energy. Positive activities like volunteer work or playing with your kids should give you a sense of getting lighter, a feeling of energy and excitement.

## Talk about it

Sometimes we don't know what we think or how we feel until we hash it over with someone else. Talking is a form of relaxation, a way to get in touch with the feelings that should drive your decisions about what's essential. Music is a universal language. I use it often to express myself. Using both my hands, playing the piano, keyboard, or organ gives me a lot of joy. I remember when my first piano arrived. I played the same song (because I could only play one song at that time) over and over again for the whole month! Five years later, I moved on to play my first Beethoven Sonata in C Minor. The second movement was so beautiful that I kept playing the first three lines for almost six hours in one sitting. That was my happiness. That was passion. You can find your own passion too. You can't really tell what you enjoy if you're flying through time and life, because then nothing is an experience; everything is on the surface. Only when you slow down, can you truly know whether something brings you deep satisfaction.

Get out your bank and credit card statements for the past 6 months. Make columns for your general spending areas (groceries, car payments, clothing, entertainment etc.). Add up how much you've spent in each category. Then ask yourself if your spending in each column is truly worth it.

Make more time for doing the things you love by simplifying your life. Try not to buy anything new for a year, except bare essentials like food, medicine, cleaning products, and underwear. In the past 15 years simplicity living has gained thousands of converts. Many books on the subject have been published such as, "The Simple Living Guide," "Circle of Simplicity," "Return to the Good Life," "Choosing Simplicity," "Real People Finding Peace and Fulfillment in a Complex World." Dozens of websites have sprung up. Simplicity to me means not having a lot of unnecessary things around yourself and not observing after what other people have. Keeping only what you need and wanting only what you need. Being satisfied with the resources at hand and not desiring more.

## Be happier with less

The desire for external wealth causes unhappiness on both a practical level and a spiritual one. In order to afford things, you have to work long hours, leaving you less time for what truly sustains you. An expensive lifestyle also limits your choice of career, forcing you to take high paying jobs that may not be fulfilling. It's hard to beat the desire for external things when we see hundreds of advertisements implying that happiness lies in a new ipod, laptop, or car. Despite those commercial messages, acquisition doesn't equal happiness.

I was once trapped in the joyless cycle of overwork and over consumption. Toiling long hours with lots of social demands kept me away from my family and the people I care about. The lucrative pay allowed me vacations around the world, dinners in fancy restaurants, expensive toys and lots of shopping. The high I got from shopping never lasted. Each time I bought something, I expected to feel better, but the emptiness inside was still there. Then, I'd buy something else. Materialism has been of form of self violence, cutting me off from what makes me happy. Now, when I do more of what matters to me, I gain deep satisfaction that renders buying and consumption less interesting. When I truly embrace simplicity I end up with riches in my soul and not in the things that I can't even take to Heaven one day!

*"I can live without money, but I cannot live without love."*
JUDY GARLAND

*"There are people who have money*
*and people who are rich."*
COCO CHANEL

4

## Lighten Your Load

How many times were we told to be like someone else, so that we could have been more handsome, beautiful, sexy, successful or desirable. One of the best vehicle advertisements I have seen in years goes like this:

"Celebrate your success…this car will take you there…where you belong…the top of the world!" Wow! What a promise and great inspirational wording. If every executive spends $80,000 on the car, definitely the profit the car company makes would take the car manufacturer to the top of the world, laughing all the way to the bank. The executive who has bought the car would have to work extra hard to pay for his expensive car just to impress others how successful he is. I was told that in the USA, the top 500 billionaires and millionaires do not actually own expensive cars. Those who drive expensive cars or stay in a $5000 a night luxury hotel room are the middle class who pretend to be super rich.

The fourth secret to finding happiness in our lives is to lighten your load. To lighten our load, we must learn to unclutter our houses. To unclutter our houses, we must learn to buy only what we need. Give away the extras to charities. Most of the time, the charities will make full use of our donations and help to unclutter our homes with the things we do not need. Let it go! We are all emotional beings, keeping memories, good or bad, for the rest of our lives. Once a year, make it a point and make an effort to throw or give away things that would make us sad or things that evoke sad memories in our lives.

When I lighten my load, unclutter my house, let it go, I minimize stress too, plus freeing up my time more to do more enriching activities that would make me happy. Less is more. Every time I travel to a new country, my life goes on living fine even with the basics like a toothbrush, toothpaste, towel, pillow, blanket, some cash and a few clothes. Those are all I need. No more, no less, so why keep and buy so many pants, shoes, sentimental spoons, little mugs, little flags to store in our houses that will only mean so much to us and not to anyone else. When I was younger, I used to keep, trade, and buy little things too whenever I traveled. I would pack them neatly into boxes and carry them home with me. Up to now, I think I have 20 or more boxes still wrapped up in the store room from each trip that I went on. The boxes are becoming useless to me now, unless I go to unwrap, pick the items one by one from each box and relive the joy of buying them. Now I prefer to look forward with hope instead of backward with regret.

Lighten up! Let it go! Free up your time, minimize stress, unclutter your home and lighten your load. Life, if you have eyes to see the whole picture, brims with meaning and purpose. It offers joy, happiness, courage, strength, and humor to cope with the inevitable negatives. For every bad and hateful act we hear about on the news, there are a thousand kindnesses that went unreported. When we get things in perspective, the almost indescribable beauty of our world will overwhelm the occasional glimpses of the ugly.

Tornadoes and violent thunderstorms are reality–but so are warm breezy summer days. Disappointment and disillusionment are realities, but so are joyful surprises. Death is an inescapable reality, but so is the miracle of birth. Live your life now; keep a clear view of reality in all its multifaceted glory, especially its pulsing, brimming, life-giving vitality. That's all you need to find happiness in your heart.

*"My life has been full of terrible misfortunes,*
*most of which never happened."*

MONTAIGNE, FRENCH PHILOSOPHER

*"Ask yourself whether you are happy*
*and you cease to be so.*
*Those who are truly happy*
*have their minds fixed on some object*
*other than their own happiness;*
*on the happiness of others,*
*on the improvement of mankind,*
*even on some art or music,*
*followed not as a means,*
*but as itself an ideal end.*
*Aiming thus at something else,*
*they find HAPPINESS by the way."*

JOHN STEWART MILL

5

## Fostering Love

"Love, love, love. Love is all you need. Love is a many splendored thing. The greatest love–Love is Forever–Loves Changes Everything–I love you truly–Forever Love. Love will take you home. Reflections of love. Everlasting love. I am in the mood for love." These are the titles of some of the most beloved songs for the past decades. Once at Kent State University, I heard a very famous speaker saying, "All over the world, people need love. With enough love, there will be no problems." Sounds very true to me.

Love will change our world just like a mother's love shapes the future of her son or daughter. How and where do we start? We can begin with caring for our family. A family can be immediate members of a family or friends around us. A Chinese proverb says, "At home we depend on our parents, in the society we depend on our friends." Once we start to care for others, we will receive much more love in return. Love is a very good investment of time. People may forget a name but will always remember a kind and loving friend. Scientific research has found a direct link between love and survival. Those who live in a circle of love would normally live more happily and longer. Being considerate, helpful, and kind to the people around us will cultivate good lasting friendships. It takes time to nurture relationships. Even a seed takes several days to grow into a tiny plant and eventually into a big tree several years later. Good friendships start and grow in the same way too.

All through my life in Malaysia, Asia, North America, and Europe, I have been blessed with the magic of friendships and love. They are like the battery charger in my life. Without them, I would be dead, not functioning and useless. The joy of friendships continues to recharge me, inspire me and lead me to go through life more meaningfully. Make the first move today to contact a long lost friend. Write a postcard, send emails or talk to someone you miss and care about today. The spirit of vocal communicating is so powerful that it enhances our lives, makes us happy and look forward to tomorrow.

My father passed away in 2003 at about 4AM in the morning in his sleep. I have often dreamed of him and talked to him in my dreams. In my heart, he has never left me.

Ever since my trip to Vancouver, I have begun to think of my home as my anchor on earth, the place where my heart is no matter where I go. It is the underlying stability that allows me to roam far, to take risks, to try new adventures, always knowing that the warm centre of my life will hold me steady.

What do you think of when you hear the word home? What images and emotions come to mind? This is something to ponder, for these images and emotions have the power to shape your life, to give it meaning, to tell you who you are. Chances are the first thing that comes to mind when you think of home, is a place. Your home is your house, your apartment, your condominium, or mobile home. It is a physical collection of space and furnishings—perhaps the sunlit dining room you love, the cramped, gloomy bathroom you hate, the kitchen that isn't quite big enough or the front bedroom that is a perfect fit for your grandmother's antique bed.

Home is your city or town, where you don't need a map to reach it, and also the countryside that surrounds it, the memorized terrain of trees and buildings—all the familiar images that define your territory on earth.

I believe the physical reality of home is a wonderful gift. Even our spiritual selves, after all, are housed in physical bodies. We all need a specific spot on this earth to call home. Certain locations speak to us, certain landscapes feel comfortable and familiar, certain places just feel like home.

As a young boy, I lived in a rented room, above a bicycle repair shop in Bruas, a tiny village in Perak, Malaysia. That room was my playground, my space, my bedroom, and my home shared with my parents and a younger sister. It was a square room with one double bed, one single metal bed which belonged to my grandfather and a baby cot for my sister. I grew up healthily in love, shaping my character and establishing excellent family ties with my small family. The street, a back lane behind the shop tells my story, my early life's history, a nest of relationships that have made me who I am today. I learned to race with friends, kids who were my age and adults who passed by on their way to work. I knew the noodle seller, the ice seller, the bun maker, and the garbage collector all by their first names!

Your circumstances, however, may be different. If you live alone, you may have to look outside your dwelling for companionship. If you are new in a community, you will need to expend some of your energy to make friends and even to find your way around.

Start by simply taking a walk. Take a walk everyday and nod or smile at the people you see regularly. From this simple base of familiarity reach out a little further. Look for people who share your interests and look for opportunities to work together as well as socialize. The sharing of a task tends to build stronger bonds of friendship and connection.

Every day of your life on this earth, the choices you make can make you constantly anchored to a warm, stable centre.

The fifth secret to happiness is to reach out, fostering love and friendships within your home and beyond.

*"The most wasted of all days is one without laughter."*
E.E. CUMMINGS

*"Love is a fruit in season at all times,*
*and within reach of every hand."*
MOTHER TERESA

6

## Put Yourself First

Maintain a healthy weight, boost your energy and get fit for life. When I was in my early twenties I did a random check on my blood pressure and got a shock to discover that I had a reading indicating that I had high blood pressure. I made efforts to modify my diet and started walking regularly. It has been more than 20 years now and I have never had any high readings of high blood pressure anymore. I eat lots of fruit and vegetables, consume less salt and drink sufficient clean water every day. Simple steps, amazing recovery. Walking every day helps me relax, maintains my desired weight and strengthens my heart and leg muscles. We have heard enough of the benefits of walking. Go on, walk today. You will enjoy the health improvement right away.

Identify a real hobby; reading, writing, painting, playing a musical instrument, gardening, watching movies, or just lying on the sofa daydreaming. These are some of the activities that you can do.

When I was in Australia in 2004, I met a very lively and happy guy who happened to be a bus driver. He was full of joy, well groomed and genuine–what's his secret of happiness? In Australia the bus schedules are excellently accurate. With the press of a button at selected bus-stops would be passengers check time of arrival of the next bus. The speaker phone would announce, "The next bus will be here in 2 minutes." Sometimes a bus may arrive early. The same bus will have to wait until the full 2 minutes before it departs. This way, any passengers would always catch the bus.

At one of the regular stops, the bus I was traveling in was early by 40 seconds. The bus driver got down from his seat, picked up something from the ground next to a tree and immediately returned to his seat and started driving again exactly 40 seconds later. I was really curious. I asked him, "Hey! Mister! What did you just pick up?" Bursting into a small laugh, he explained, "Oh! That was a used generator (the size of a tennis ball) which the electrician left behind to be picked up by a recycling truck." The electrician had just replaced a new generator and left the old one there. The bus driver concluded that he has been collecting about 800 generators of all sizes for the past 3 years and that gives him a lot of pleasure in driving the bus every day and it shows!

He is constantly looking for used generators which cost him nothing and that gives him the joy and determination to get up every morning to drive the bus in the best manner he could. This is his secret to happiness.

So many of us lose the simple joy life brings. We can be thankful for blue or rainy skies. We decide what makes us happy and as long as we stick to our principles of happiness, I do not see any reasons why we are not happy.

Regain control of your life, pamper yourself once in a while, maintain a healthy weight, get fit for life and boost your energy by breathing in slowly everyday. Inhale through your nostrils and exhale through your mouth. Breathing correctly and effectively supplies enough oxygen to our lungs, brains, and cells.

Celebrate yourself. This doesn't mean adopting a selfish outlook or focusing only on your own needs. It does mean doing everything you can to realize the inherent privilege of waking up every morning, rejoicing in the fact that you have a functioning body. Regardless of its failings, it still performs its job in wonderful ways. It carries you around, connects you to the world through its senses, and enables you to process the information you receive. It carries on the basic functions of sustaining life–heartbeat, breathing, di-gestion–with surprising little fuss, especially considering the abuse it sometimes takes. Even if your body differs from the standard model–if, for example, it cannot walk or hear–it still offers you countless options for joy and usefulness.

Put yourself first.

*"I want things to be the best they can be. I want greatness."*
DEMI MOORE

*"Trust in what you love, continue to do it,*
*and it will take you where you need to go."*
NATALIE GOLDBERG

7

## Gain Financial Freedom

This subject has been the hottest topic since mankind invented money. Thousands of books have been written on this favorite topic. More than 50% of the seminars which are conducted on this planet talk directly or indirectly enthusiastically about these three words–GAIN FINANCIAL FREEDOM.

Many companies around the globe use these high profile words to attract customers, partners, and agents. What exactly is "Gain Financial Freedom?" to me, it means go on living with life without any worry about money. Is it possible? How many people have done it? The answer lies in your heart. How much do you need to live until 85 years old?

A financial planner will tell you that you will need a minimum of half a million to sustain your lifestyle when you retire to beat the inflation rate. Generally, fear is there, everyone is afraid to lose something if they cannot keep up with their current income in 20, 30, or 40 year's time. This chapter is not trying to teach you how much to earn now so that you can retire rich and still live in style. I am trying to impress upon you the value of "rich" and show you how you could find the secrets of happiness through some simple steps you can adopt today. Interested?

My first recommendation is reducing your debt. Pay off your credit card bills every month in full. Do not let any credit card's debt go on beyond 3 months. If you cannot cut down credit card expenses, you have to cut away the plastic!

Secondly, do not withdraw money from the ATM. Spend what you have and when you have the money. Withdrawing from an ATM will surely drain your hard earned money away faster than your deposits.

Do not gamble. When you stop gambling you have already won. All the card games and slot machines are meant to profit the dealers and the machines' owner, not us. The chance of winning is too slim. The majority lose. That is why casinos all over the world are getting bigger each day. Not only bigger but brighter to attract more losers! Do not be trapped. Know your limit and play for fun if you wish to.

Settle your loan quicker by putting down more money each time. Let's say your home loan repayment is $600 a month for 25 years. Put in $650, you will find that you could finish paying the loan several years sooner. If you put in $800 a month, instead of the usual $600 as month, you could finish paying much sooner than you think and save lots of money in interest.

Move to a smaller house. Drive a smaller car. Very soon, you will gain financial freedom too. This is the best kept secret to happiness–debt free. Consider moving to a smaller town. The air is fresher anyway, less traffic, and less stress. The kids would be happier too in a smaller town's school–less competition and better attention from the teachers. They will have more space to roam, to grow, and to breathe! What are you waiting for?

Work smart instead of work hard. Leverage your time and earn more to free up your time. Work less. Use your imagination. Your mind is more powerful than you think.

### How to earn an extra million in your lifetime?

The real key is to keep socking away the money. Let the numbers whisper their silent but relentless message. Consistency. Day in, day out–Save–Invest–Save–Invest. It might be boring. It might be dull. It might be hard to do. No matter. Just do it.

The sooner you start, the richer you are immediately. If you save just a $1 a day. For 54 years with 5% interest, you would accumulate $100,000; with 10% interest you would accumulate $1 million. Similarly, if you save $20 a day for 54 years, with 5% interest, you would accumulate $2 million and with 10% interest, your $20 a day savings would accumulate to $20 million! Not bad at all.

Your moneymaking will be much more successful and meaningful if you have a clear purpose. If it's just to make a lot of money, you may find yourself one day with a lot of money, wondering, "It this all there is?"

The Ford Foundation was established in 1936, yet decades later is still giving away more than $100 million a year to needy causes. No matter what your attitude toward the wealth of Bill Gates, the Rockefellers, or the Gettys, you've got to admit that hundreds of thousands of people (even you) are benefiting each day from the legacy of these great money makers. The fruits from their money trees continue to bless the world.

### Interesting Facts About Money

The man who started IKEA divides his day into ten minute sections. He says, "Ten minutes, once gone are gone for good. Divide your life into ten minute units, and don't waste even a minute."

You don't have to fill your time rushing about in order to use your time wisely. Bill Gates–the world's top charity donor–said his staff could spend two hours gazing into space, as long as their minds were working and Albert Einstein came up with the theory of relativity in his mind without paper or pen. He only wrote it down later.

It's said that money is the root of all evil. It doesn't have to be. Money can be used for good. Harvard, the wealthiest university in the USA started with a few books and $350. IKEA started in a garden shed. The man who dreamed up McDonalds started life selling paper cups. At 52, he created McDonalds and his company now gives $50 million a year for charity. Money can be a force for good. But you don't need to be rich to do rich. Children collect empty coke tins or sell old newspapers to raise money for good causes.

Gaining financial freedom means much more than earning a lot of money and living happily ever after. It means

34

you can choose to be very rich and you can choose to be such a powerful steward over your forest of money trees that they can produce fruit to feed generations of people long after you are gone.

*"You make a living by what you get,*
*you make a life by what you give."*

WINSTON CHURCHILL, BRITISH PRIME MINISTER

*"What I gave, I have.*
*What I spent, I had.*
*What I had left, I lost."*

CHRISTOPHER CHAPMAN, 17TH CENTURY PHILANTHROPIST

8

## Three Roads to Happiness

When positive psychologists talk about happiness, what they mean is a sense of deep contentment. There are 3 routes to achieving contentment and the most satisfied people pursue all three.

The first one is the PLEASANT LIFE, full of pleasure, joy and good times.

The second one is the ENGAGED LIFE, in which you lose yourself to some passion or activity experiencing flow.

The third is the MEANGINFUL LIFE. It may not have many high moments or blissful immersion, but it is packed with purpose.

One way to see what makes people happy is to see what happy people like. When researchers looked at the traits shared by volunteers, who scored high on measures of happiness, one floated to the top: the ability to love and be loved.

Relationships with other people are what make us happiest. Our connections to others are the foundation of humanity. Love doesn't necessarily mean romance. I'm talking about close relationships with other people, friends, parents, and children. Humans are social creatures, when we're engaged with our fellows, we are happiest. We were not created to sit alone in front of a computer all day.

If your top character strength isn't love, don't think you're short changing yourself on the relationship front.

Using your strengths, whatever they are, will likely connect you to others too. Take expressing gratitude. Gratitude increases the morale of the person who receives it. That person tries to be better and your relationship with him or her becomes stronger and you both feel happier.

Curiosity, as well, links us to others. You meet someone, ask questions and the other person begins to reveal things about himself or herself. You ask more and the other person feels accepted. Curiosity builds a relationship too. And remember, relationships with other people are what make us happiest (the 8th secret to happiness).

*"You have not lived a perfect day,*
*even though you have earned your money,*
*unless you have done something*
*for someone who will never be able to repay you."*
RUTH SMELTZER

*"I am not bound to win, I am bound to be true.*
*I am not bound to succeed,*
*but I am bound to live up to the light that I have."*
ABRAHAM LINCOLN

9

## Light a Fresh Candle

Creativity, you might say, is my business. As a professional piano player, I make my living from dreaming up worlds that never really existed and bringing them to life on the piano. Creativity is a tool of my trade, just as surely as my fingers and breathing techniques. In a sense, it is also my stock in trade, because I make a living selling the fruits of my creativity.

Creativity has everything to do with the way you live, because creativity is the essence of your heritage as a human being. It's impossible for you not to be creative, at least when it comes to your potential. Your creation doesn't have to be a poem or a sonata or a marble statue or any kind of traditional artistic work. Creativity can also produce a salmon mousse, a jet propulsion system, a crossword puzzle, a striking new hair design, or a Japanese garden. Creativity can shape or reshape an entire life.

It's the gift that enables us to solve our problems, to move from Point A to Point B or C or Z, to explore the full depth and potential of the human experience.

My cousin-in-law is a very successful barber in Singapore. He calls himself Chief Artistic Director. His fine and unique hair styling talent has made him one of the most in demand hair stylists in Singapore. People love his charisma and his ability to create a fresh look every time he cuts someone's hair off, reshapes it and makes his customers look glamorous, neat and beautiful.

Every time you attempt to solve a problem, you're being creative. Every time you try a new path, invent a new approach, craft a new object, you are rearranging the raw material of your life into something new—and that's the essence of creativity. You are using your mind, your imagination, your hands, and your spiritual connection to make something that has never existed before in that particular combination.

Creativity is what separates us from other species—an ongoing way of emulating the Creator Himself, who when He finished His task about and said, "It is good."

With every creative act, you light a fresh candle for a darkened world—and that in itself is a powerful source of happiness for your life.

One of the most fruitful "creative" sources in my life is people. I love to spend time with those who are in the process of putting new things together. I find my mind and creativity stimulated by conversations with other musicians, interactions with writers, and conferences with business people. When I travel around the globe, I love to visit art museums, talk to the chefs at restaurants I visit, and simply enjoy conversations with taxi drivers. Taxi drivers can provide a lot of information on the city you are in. Ask them about their lives, their families, and they will share with you all they know about the city, where to shop, where to stay, and where to avoid! Such conversations often provide both energy and ideas to fuel my creative projects.

If you want to live more creatively and more happily, you'll surround yourself with a number of things. You'll look at them, touch them, smell them, listen to them, and think about them. When your heart and mind are full, you'll be well on the way toward awakening the joy of creativity.

The ninth secret to happiness is to explore your creativity, let you and your work inspire people to be better in what they do. In other words, happiness is a light and we become the source—the candle.

*"If you do things well, do them better.*
*Be daring, be first, be different, be just."*
ANITA RODDICK

*"Optimism brings with it many benefits:*
*lower stress, better health, greater confidence,*
*better and longer relationships,*
*and more happiness and fulfillment."*
JOHN TRAUTH

KC FOONG

10

## Second Journey

This will be the final secret to happiness in Section One of this book. By no means is it the end. There are a lot more ways to happiness out there, waiting to be explored, embraced and enjoyed. To proceed to the next phase of your life, you will need to challenge yourself in a bigger way. You may need to leave your present comfort zone, so to speak, for a time, travel to an unknown foreign place, or take up a new career. You are on a new journey now, your second journey. Along the way, as you stay true to yourself, you will begin to feel a new found sense of empowerment. That's total freedom. That's our tenth secret to happiness.

### Where could you go for an hour?

Try to list at least 10 possible places where you have one hour of uninterrupted solitude. Could you go to a park, library, bathroom, car, garden, the zoo, a museum, hiking, biking, a book shop, fishing, kayaking, or a room of your own?

### Where could you go overnight or for a weekend?

Keep your focus on the place, list 5 or more. Too often we paralyze ourselves worrying about the hurdles before we even allow ourselves to envision the possibility of a retreat. Making a plan gives you power and a feeling of power gives you hope. Hope gives you space to think about beautiful and exciting things. You feel happy already. React to your peace, the secret spot, the special moment, noticing all that offered you—

What do you hear, smell, or see?

What are you yearning for?

What are you seeking?

What must you eliminate from your everyday life?

What do you need more of?

We actually possess everything we need to move forward. Each of us has inherited all the bold vision, the courage, the compassion, and the integrity to repair our lives and well-being. These sturdy roots may have been neglected and hidden under years of accumulated dirt, misunderstanding and social conformity.

Real change comes with time and involves the strength of recalling our history, without which we can never recover ourselves. Gather your energy and embark on your second journey. The second journey of self discovery which I will explain in another 10 different chapters in Section Two of this book.

> *"It is not so much that we are afraid of change,*
> *or so in love with the way things are –*
> *it's the place in between that we fear."*
> MARILYN FERGUSON, AUTHOR, POET

> *"Challenges are what make life interesting;*
> *overcoming them is what makes life meaningful."*
> JOSHUA J. MARINE

> *"Ability is what you're capable of doing,*
> *motivation determines what you do,*
> *attitude determines how you will do it."*
> LOU HOLTZ

> *"You measure the size of the accomplishment*
> *by the obstacles you had to overcome, to reach your goals."*
> BOOKER T. WASHINGTON

> *"Within each of us is a hidden store of determination.*
> *Determination to keep us in a race when all seems lost."*
> ROGER DAWSON

*"We all have the ability. The difference is how we use it."*
STEVIE WONDER

*"Happiness is good health and a bad memory."*
INGRID BERGMAN

*"But what is happiness,*
*except the simple harmony*
*between a man and the life he leads."*
ALBERT CAMUS

*"Living in the moment relaxes us, lowers our stress level,*
*and is crucial for living happily."*
(*THE POWER OF NOW* BY ECKHART TOLLE)

*"Vision without action is hallucination."*
ATTRIBUTION UNKNOWN

SECTION II

## 10 SECRETS OF SELF DISCOVERY

1

# Who Am I? (Part I)

Remember who you were when you were at your best? What generally makes you feel fulfilled? Think back to those times or situations in which you have been most creative. They can be from school, work, hobbies, your art work, building a cupboard, helping a person in need, public speaking, sleeping–wherever you have felt that you were completely satisfied to be doing what you were doing in the way your were doing it.

Come up with ten such situations and write them down below.

**What I Was Doing When I Was at My Best**

a _____

b _____

c _____

d _____

e _____

f _____

g _____

h _____

i_____

j_____

Have you done it? For many of us, identifying the happiest times of our lives can be very natural. Sharing with a small group is even more interesting.

I was happiest during my childhood when my parents spent time with me, going to a park, playing badminton, or just talking to me, especially when I was ill. If you are blessed with children, show the same love to your kids. Love grows brains. Love helps children to learn to cope with stress and handle their feelings all through life. Love teaches children how to be loving and caring people. In return, we experience love and happiness, by caring and loving not only our own children, but other children as well.

If you are a critical thinker, to come up with your happier memories may be especially challenging. Instead, try this experience as a reverse situation you would describe as your life's low points. This is to examine what absences or situations in your life created bad feelings, whether physical or psychological. You may then be able to work backward to create your list of what conditions encourage you to feel happy and creative, your satisfaction highlights.

**Worst Experiences in Life**

a _____

b _____

c _____

d _____

e _____

f_____

g _____

h _____

i_____

j_____

KC FOONG

After you are done with the best and worst experience, now list down 3 specific moments when you were so involved in a project, accomplishing a task or solving a problem that you do not even realize you have been working for an extended time.

## My Selected Happy Moments

a _____

b _____

c _____

How did it feel to be there? What were you doing? What are you trying to accomplish? Who were you with? Was it necessary that they were there?

What were the results?

Now write your stories and recall your selected happy moments here.

## My Story

_____
_____
_____
_____
_____
_____
_____
_____
_____
_____
_____
_____
_____
_____
_____

Let me summarize some of the actions which could make us happy

a   Working with hands.
b   Solving a problem.
c   Completing a project.
d   Being your own boss.
e   Negotiating to buy a car.
f   Learning to maintain a car.
g   Wake up early to breathe in fresh air.
h   Researching and organizing a project.
i   Playing on the piano.
j   Strumming the guitar.
k   Blowing your saxophone.
l   Creating rhythms on the drum set.
m   Producing beautiful melodies on your violin.
n   Bake a cake for a friend.
o   Watch a favorite movie.
p   Lying on the beach with your favorite book.
q   Sleep late till 1:00PM.
r   Praising God in church.
s   Cycling in the park.
t   Have an excellent haircut.
u   Bought a favorite dress on sale, half price.
v   Obedient children.
w   Understanding boss.
x   Loving spouse.
y   Flying a kite on a windy day.
z   Fishing with a group of friends.

Read your story to yourself or to a small group in a workshop. These are the things you are interested in, what you like to do. They also tell you what your goals are or what you are trying to achieve. Get to know yourself much better and you will soon discover your own secrets of your happiness. They could be—

a   Having plenty to do.
b   Having nothing to do.
c   Have to make clear cut decisions.
d   Have others be direct and logical.
e   Knowing exactly what to do.

f   Being able to work without interruption.
g   Being trusted.
h   Using a variety of skills.
i   Have others encourage your feelings.
j   Feeling free from constant social demands.
k   Having a self determined schedule.
l   Enjoy individualized rewards.
m   Knowing who is in charge.
n   Go to work when you want.
o   No traffic jams.
p   No rude drivers.
q   No rude customers.
r   No gossiping in the office.
s   A bright sunny day.
t   A cloudy, rainy day!
u   A breezy summer day.
v   A cold winter morning.
w   A beautiful spring afternoon.
x   A relaxing autumn evening.
y   A hot, sunny tropical day on the beach.
z   A cool, misty day in the forest.

What needs did you find gratifying or satisfying from your memory? When are you most happy and the clock seems to stand still or goes by swiftly. Were you—
a   Demonstrating independence?
b   Contributing to a feeling of communicating?
c   Working alone?
d   Working with one other person?
e   Working with a group?
f   Working for self gain?
g   Working to be important to others?
h   Working for yourself?
i   Working for someone else?
j   Working for an organization?
k   Directing and controlling the situation?
l   Playing an indispensable role?
m   Carrying out orders?
n   Directing others?
o   Helping others?

p   Learning something new?
q   Being creative?
r   Influencing others?
s   Enjoying good food alone?
t   Enjoying good food with friends?
u   Standing on top of a mountain?
v   Racing with your dog to play catch?
w   Writing a book?
x   Singing your favorite karaoke songs?
y   Playing golf competitively?
z   Playing golf leisurely?

You should now have a very good idea of your interest, your style, your needs, and your skills. You also should have a better understanding of the situations and environments in which you shine. My good Malaysian friend, Larry, has always been reminding me to shine. To shine is a powerful courage. I have a much better understanding of myself. What about you? What areas of your life are you called to shine?

Let's move on to the next chapter to further discover yourself and find out what are you made of and made for.

*"Everyone has talent.*
*What is rare is the courage to follow that talent*
*to the dark place where it leads."*
ERICA JONG

*"The moment somebody says, 'this is risky,'*
*is the moment it becomes attractive to me."*
KATE CAPSHAW

2

# Who Am I? (Part II)

I first came to know about the four temperaments of human beings at 16 from my English teacher, Miss Ling Kay Bin. As far as I remember, she was the first school teacher who taught me to improve in my English language and I am forever grateful to her.

There are four main characteristics of human beings on this planet. Some of us have characteristic behavior in 2, 3, or all the four temperaments. Knowing yourself will help identify your strengths and weaknesses. Many international corporations around the globe conduct the temperament analysis to choose their best managers and CEOs.

Do you see where you belong?

| IMPLEMENTERS | COMMUNICATORS |
|---|---|
| Task Oriented | People Oriented |
| Organizer | Works with People to get results |
| Delegates | Acts Direct |
| Acts Direct | Feels Sensitive |
| Feels Direct | |

| ADMINISTRATORS | PLANNERS |
|---|---|
| System Oriented | Idea Oriented |
| Controller | Planner |
| Uses system to get results | Uses ideas to get results |
| Acts Sensitive | Acts Sensitive |
| Feels Direct | Feels Sensitive |

| IMPLEMENTERS LIKE TO: | COMMUNICATORS LIKE TO: |
|---|---|
| Build | Sell and promote |
| Organize | Persuade |
| See a finished product | Motivate people |
| Solve a practical problem | Counsel or teach |
| Work through people | Work with people |
| (You like practical, technical, objective, hands-on and problem-solving types of responsibilities and professions). | (You like persuasive, selling, promotional and group-contact types of responsibilities and professions). You prefer to work where things get done with a minimum of thought and where persuasion is well received by others. |
| You prefer to perform your responsibilities in a manner that is action oriented and practical. You prefer to work where things happen quickly and results are seen immediately. | |

| ADMINISTRATORS LIKE TO: | PLANNERS LIKE TO: |
|---|---|
| Schedule activities<br>Do detailed work<br>Keep close control<br>Work with numbers<br>Work with systems<br>(You like organized, detail oriented, predictable and objective types of responsibilities and professions).<br>You prefer to work in a manner that is orderly, planned to meet a schedule, where things get done with a minimum of interpretation and unexpected change. | Plan activities<br>Deal with abstraction<br>Think of new approaches<br>Innovate<br>Work with ideas<br>(You like creative, humanistic, thoughtful and quiet types of responsibilities and professions).<br>You prefer to work in a manner which is supportive and helpful to others with minimum confrontation and have time to think before acting. |

These are more examples where we might belong. Once you find out more intimately about your preference, your style, your interest, and your inspirations, you will seek passionately the secrets of happiness in your life.

| IMPLEMENTERS | | |
|---|---|---|
| Interest | Styles | Preferred Environment |
| Doing<br>Building<br>Implementing<br>Organizing<br>Producing<br>Delegating<br>Leading | Straightforward<br>Assertive<br>Logical<br>Personable<br>Authoritative<br>Friendly<br>Direct<br>Resourceful | Self Structured<br>High Pressure<br>Hierarchical<br>Production Oriented<br>Competitive |

| COMMUNICATORS | | |
|---|---|---|
| **Interest** | **Styles** | **Preferred Environment** |
| Motivating | Spontaneous | Team Oriented |
| Mediating | Talkative | Adventurous |
| Selling | Personal | Informal |
| Influencing | Enthusiastic | Innovative |
| Consensus Building | Convincing | Big Picture Oriented |
| Persuading | Risk Taking | Varied |
| Debating | Competitive | |
| Delegating Authority | Genuine | |

By listing good qualities, you're training yourself to reverse your focus from what you did wrong to what you did right. You're emphasizing your strengths and that seems to change the way you feel. Using your character strengths helps compensate for weaknesses that otherwise can interfere with happiness.

| ADMINISTRATORS | | |
|---|---|---|
| **Interest** | **Styles** | **Preferred Environment** |
| Ordering | Cautious | Predictable |
| Numbering | Structured | Established |
| Scheduling | Loyal | Controlled |
| Systematizing | Systematic | Measurable |
| Preserving | Solitary | Orderly |
| Maintaining | Methodical | |
| Measuring | Organized | |
| Specifying Details | Strict | |

| PLANNERS | | |
|---|---|---|
| **Interest** | **Styles** | **Preferred Environment** |
| Abstracting | Insightful | Cutting Edge |
| Theorizing | Reflective | Informally Paced |
| Designing | Selectively Sociable | Organized in private Offices |
| Writing | Creative | Low Key |
| Reflecting | Thoughtful | Future Oriented |
| Originating | Emotional | |
| Composing | Imaginative | |
| Inventing | Sensitive | |

You are now developing a vocabulary to describe yourself in order to discover who you really are. As you look through the descriptions of the tables above, you will definitely recognize which box or boxes you belong to. Remembering and knowing your strengths and weaknesses, your interest and style will guide you toward your best and most productive happy moments.

> *"Your worth consists in what you are*
> *and not in what you have."*
> THOMAS A. EDISON

3

# Who Am I? (Part III)

**I Describe My Interest**

a _____

b _____

c _____

d _____

e _____

**II What strengths would I like to develop, based on my interest, style, and temperament?**

a _____

b _____

c _____

d _____

e _____

**III How do I seek opportunities to do this?**

a _____

b _____

c _____

d _____

e _____

I believe by now, you have simplified your life enough to know what you want and where to get it. Always remember life is not just getting all that you want but rather happiness, joy, peace, and love. We are just travellers on earth. Please remember to smell the flowers, water some plants, pluck some weeds, and take things lightly.

*"Tell me what you love and I'll tell you who you are."*
ATTRIBUTION UNKNOWN

4

# Who Are the Happy People?

**Happy People like Themselves.**

For the past 25 years, I have been actively talking and interviewing and meeting people wherever my travel took me. I have come to know many happy people. They are ordinary people like you and me. The first characteristic and the most outstanding one is happy people like themselves.

Mike lives in Switzerland. He loves swimming, skiing, hiking, playing the drums, and even cooking. He was in Sabah recently for his diving trip and captured a lot of underwater photographs of the marine fish, turtles, coral reefs and even giant turtles and sea snakes! He is a very happy guy and has a lot of other interests too. I had the chance to play music with his band in Zurich in 2005. On the drums he invented several cool beats. He loves watching himself playing the drums, gets even more excited when the audience are listening. By the way, he looks 10 years younger than his actual age.

Ben is a very successful fashion entrepreneur in Toronto, Canada. He loves beautiful women, fashion, and his work. At the young age of 21, he has already got 200 female models working for him. He travels to New York regularly to make contacts, loves his exposure and is highly sought after as a top fashion organizer and consultant. Blue seems to be his favorite color...usually a light blue collar shirt and a dark blue jacket with blue jeans accompany him to work or play. He loves his busy appointments and hectic schedules. He is one of the most happy men on the planet!

## Happy People are Hopeful

Hopeful people spend their time thinking, planning, and dreaming about beautiful things, memories and events. Herbert has been a Christian youth leader for more than 30 years in all parts of Asia and North America. I remember asking him in 1986, "What makes you motivated to do your job well?" He replied with a smile, "Seeing the young people grow under my guidance and serving God. Young people motivate me to give my best to them. God humbles my heart to experience joy."

In 1992 Herbert invited me to Chicago, USA, to participate in a multi church music festival in the summer. He was well loved by the people around him. He has always put people first, listens to their problems, prays with them, guides them toward God's mighty plans, and puts all his trust and hope in an eternal God. I admire him for his constant faithfulness in serving and helping people, and his simple happy life in Petaling Jaya, Malaysia.

He always hopes for the best in others, the organizations he is involved in, and has touched hundreds of thousands of souls who have come to know him personally. Herbert is really one blessed man, doing what he loves the most. That is his calling. That is his passion. He knows who holds the future for him and his family. I am really glad to be a part of his growing ministry around the world–touching hearts and changing lives, wherever he goes.

## Happy People are Outgoing

Kee works for himself, is extremely outgoing and feels very positive about himself, his career and his living environment. Through his daring but smart moves, he has invested in a number of properties without any money down. He plans very well for his future, enjoying life at the same time. He seems to know everyone on the street. He makes friends easily, is friendly, genuine and straightforward. He frees his heart from hatred and his mind from worries. He lives day to day, happy all the time.

Vince is a store manager, working long hours in the day and delivering papers from 2:30AM to 6:00AM, 7 days a week. Most people would break down and give up, but his perseverance keeps him going. He gets along with almost anybody, is outgoing and helpful.

Kee and Vince, 2 guys who live 30,000 miles apart have very similar characters. Both have strong wills to succeed, invest for their families, are hard working and feel happy most of the time. They have no time to feel sad or depressed. Both are successful in their chosen careers, work many more hours than any guys that I have ever known. Life to them is a journey to be enjoyed. Both are my real good friends in 2 different parts of the world. Joy can be anywhere in this world and be happy too.

## Happy People Believe They Choose their Destinies

In my life, traveling here and there, I have come to know many authors, life coaches, business coaches, and instructors in various fields such as martial arts, creative arts, dance, yoga, music, marketing and so on. These people know what they want in their lives. Regardless of the income levels, they are really happy people who believe they choose their destinies.

In their area of training, they tend to give more and expect less. They are always in touch with the latest news and technology to stay competitive in their chosen fields. They surround themselves with all the objects of art and beauty that they are capable of using and appreciating. They constantly develop their minds and unfold their souls. They are highly effective because their bodies are living fully in every function; physical, mental, and spiritual. I can't find anyone who is happier than they are, even though some may have inherited millions, live in big mansions and have all the money in the world to buy anything in this world.

Happiness is from within. My friend in Shanghai, China, Tien Lee, told me that the happiest people he has known are the farmers who live in interior China. The farmers are happy just to have food on the table everyday with no money, no bank account, no proper housing facilities, and no entertainment. They sleep at 7:00PM, wake up at 5:00AM every morning to work on the farms. Many live till 120! No signs of disease, just old age. They are the happiest people on earth!

5

# Life's Greatest Lesson

*"We must make the choices that enable us to fulfill the deepest capacities of our real selves."*
THOMAS MERTON

Celebrating triumphs of the human spirit, especially when it involves personal growth, is one of the great rewards of life. I am not telling anyone how to live his or her life. I just hope some of my own struggles and the discoveries that resulted from will deepen your understanding about how life works and what's essential for a life with purpose, meaning and joy. And I hope that they'll be things that work for you too.

One of my great joys of life is knowing that there's always room for increased self awareness and personal growth. We can be better, happier, and wiser at any time we choose.

*"Purpose is the place where your deep gladness meets the world's need."*
FREDERICK BUECHNER

Millions of people are complaining about their lot, disgusted with life and the way things are going, not realizing that there is a power which they possess which will permit them to take a new lease on life. Dare you recognize this power and begin to use it, you can change your entire life and make it the way you would like to have it... filled with joy.

The greatest power that a person possesses is the power to choose. Wisdom is the result when we learn to make better choices.

Choose to be humble—
   i Humble people don't think they know everything.
  ii Humble people don't think they're always right.
 iii Humble people don't brag.
 iv Humble people don't judge others.

As wise as they are—
   i Humble people treat others with respect.
  ii Humble people are thankful.
 iii Humble people are genuine.
 iv Humble people want to learn and become better.

Being prepared to set aside old notions and be taught by life is learning humility. Once we humble ourselves, we see the greatness in other people. Once we see the greatness in other people, we will start to imagine how much we have to learn. This is a very simple and basic secret to happiness.

Ability to appreciate others, to learn more and to see the beauty of God's creation, I have observed that after a harsh winter season, I could see on some trees in Vancouver, the flowers bloom first. Several weeks later, in order for the tiny new leaves to uncurl, the flowers fade away to give space for the tiny new leaves. These tiny new leaves grow bigger and greener every day until they fill up the whole tree in the summer to become a big healthy tree. When autumn arrives, the strong and green big leaves have to die, first by turning into red, yellow, brown and eventually drop from the tree. This is the process of nature to let the tree live. Both flowers and leaves come and go as seasons change. As life goes on, we should be humble enough to step down when somebody stronger and younger comes along. No point fighting over a top spot.

*"Meaning is strength.*
*Our survival may depend on our seeking and finding it."*
VIKTOR FRANKL

*"This is true joy in life, the being used for a purpose recognized by yourself as a mighty one."*
GEORGE BERNARD SHAW

KC FOONG

6

# Patience in a High Speed Society

*"If I have ever made any valuable discoveries,
it has been owing more to patient attention
than to any other talent."*
ISAAC NEWTON

Learn the art of patience. Apply discipline to your thoughts when they become anxious. Impatience breeds anxiety, fear, discouragement, and failure. These are all the opposite of happiness. On the contrary, patience creates confidence, decisiveness, and a rational outlook, which can eventually lead to success.

Think of all the wonderful people who've been kind, understanding, and tolerant when you were being less than your best. Where would you be without them? Doesn't it make you want to work on becoming more patient with the people around you?

*"Genius is eternal patience."*
MICHELANGELO

The more we cultivate patience, the happier and more peaceful we are, even if things don't always turn out the way we want. Patience helps us make wiser choices and makes us more loving toward other people. In short, patience makes us better persons. The greatest rewards are healthier relationships, higher quality work, and peace of mind.

*"Everything comes to him who hustles while he waits."*
THOMAS EDISON

One of the most patient men I have got to know dearly was my own father. All through my childhood and adult life, he has never shown his temper to me or any other member of my family. When I wanted to eat my favorite snacks, "Loh Mai Kai," at 8:30PM, he would patiently cycle to a nearby Chinese restaurant, "Sing Hong Sang," to buy the food that I requested.

When I was a young boy, sometimes in the afternoon, if I wanted to play badminton, he would play badminton with me under the hot tropical sun without any hesitation. He waited patiently for me to grow up. I can feel his love all through my life even now. Knowing my father is one of my best roads to happiness. No one can take away the joy of being his son.

I am sure all of you have great fathers and mothers. Cherish and love them while they are alive. You will find happiness in loving your loved ones. This is the greatest reward in love. Be grateful, be thankful, above all, be patient, especially in loving someone.

*"Patience and perseverance have a magical effect,*
*before which, difficulties and obstacles vanish."*
JOHN QUINCY ADAMS

*"Love is patience, love is kind..."*
THE BIBLE

7

# Something Worthwhile

There's something to celebrate everyday. Look for the good–you'll find it.

Happiness is a wonderful emotion. It helps people see the big picture and they like what they see. They accept life the way it is, they focus on the good and they find reasons to celebrate. It is closely related to thankfulness, which is both an attitude and a habit. The happiest people in the world are not the ones who have the most, but the ones who appreciate the most. They're grateful to be alive.

When we lead lives of honesty and integrity, when we're compassionate, kind, and helpful, when we contribute to our communities or to worthy causes, when we admit our weaknesses and challenge ourselves to grow out of them, when we forgive others, and when we honor God by living as He asks us to, we make a difference in the world and we experience feelings of happiness and a joy on a daily basis.

## More Steps to Happiness—

Develop and maintain a positive attitude. Look for the good, find it, celebrate it. Always be thankful.

Practice the Golden Rule. Treat other people with respect and kindness. Always have something good to say.

Give of your time and your resources. Serve your community and help others. Contribute to making the world a better place.

Make integrity the cornerstone of your life.

Honor the rules, play fair and be honest.

Maintain a standard of excellence. Work hard at everything you do. Always give your best.

Make learning a lifetime pursuit. Grow, improve and renew yourself daily.

Enjoy life. Remember you need to play and have fun. Even more important, remember to laugh!

Be mindful of the needs of your body, and your mind. Eat well, sleep well and exercise.

Give your life meaning and purpose. Set lifetime goals.

Be humble. Always be aware of your weaknesses and limitations. Improve upon them.

Be patient. Think before you talk and think before you act. Patience is part of wisdom.

Learn to forgive. Be at peace with others whenever possible.

Think with an open mind. Use your imagination to see the opportunities and the possibilities around you.

Enhance your spiritual life. Read the scriptures and honor their teachings. Pray daily.

Make time for your priorities. Understand that time is your most valuable resource.

Say "Yes" to life. Have the courage to face up to hardship and disappointment.

Cook a meal today–cater to your own taste, the right amount of salt, the right texture, and the right mood to serve your meal to others or yourself.

Look at fish swim. They don't seem to stop. Their bodies are always in motion, always happy.

Be a listening ear. Lots of people are lonely out there. Listen to them and be their lifelong friend.

Draw, play, paint or practice a musical instrument. Attend a concert or invite a friend to a concert.

Write a journal. Write a poem. Write a short note. Writing is one of the best therapies to achieve peace.

Peace at the end leads to contentment and happiness.

KC FOONG

*"You are never too old to set another goal
or to dream a new dream."*

C.S. LEWIS

*"The difference between the impossible and the possible
lies in a person's determination."*

TOMMY LASORDA

8

## Why Are We Here?

Everyone has daily routines which help provide structure and comfort to each day. It's important that we respect each other's individual needs. Modern life is rich and complex. We have so many more choices today about how to live.

With this freedom comes a depth of experience and a greater understanding of life and love. Social and economic changes have altered so much. Today, women are in the workplace in every capacity. Both husband and wife can have a career. Or women can work and men stay home. Delayed childbirth allows older women and men to start families which can both limit and expand the possibilities of family life.

We learn that we can never control someone else's behavior and when people want us not to be true to ourselves and push us to engage in their anger, all we can do is remain calm. There are no prescriptions that we can hand out that will appease the other person. But we can stop in our tracks, take deep breaths and listen to become better informed. Do not indulge poor behavior by yelling back, even though this may be your immediate, self protective instinct.

Ask any number of people to describe a moment of perfect happiness, Some will talk about moments of deep peace experienced in a harmonious natural setting, of a forest dappled in sunshine, of a mountain's summit, looking out across a vast horizon, of the shore of a tranquil lake, of a night walk through snow under a starry sky, of a walk in the forest on a rainy day, and so on. Others will refer to a long awaited event, an exam they scored with flying colors, a sporting victory, meeting someone they've longed to meet, the birth of a child. Still others will speak of a moment of tranquility with their family or a loved one, or of having made someone else happy.

The common factor to all these experiences would seem to be the momentary disappearance of inner conflicts. The person feels in harmony with the world and with himself. Someone enjoying such an experience, such as walking through a serene wilderness, has no particular expectations beyond this simple act of walking. He simply is, here and now, free and open.

For just a moment, thoughts of the past are suppressed, the mind is not burdened with plans for the future, and the present moment is liberated from all mental constructs. This moment of respite, from which all sense of emotional urgency has vanished, is experienced as one of profound peace. For someone who has achieved a goal, completed a task, or won a victory, the tension they have long carried with them relaxes. The ensuing sense of release is felt as a deep calm, free from all expectations and fear. I call it a magic moment, a state of grace.

I remember one afternoon. I was sitting on the beach of Long Island named Long Beach. The year was 1990 and it was bright and sunny. There was no one there except me, admiring miles and miles of white sandy beach.

All of a sudden, the wind blew so hard that some sand got into my eyes. That was when I looked up to the sky. To my shock, there was a long and black snake-shaped cloud forming fast, right above me and it seemed to cover the entire sky rapidly, blocking the sunshine and causing big waves to pound on the beach. I was terrified. It looked as if the world was going to end. I didn't know anything about Tsunamis then.

As fast as I could, I ran back to my car and started driving away from the scary clouds and monster waves. As I was driving away in a great hurry, the clouds started to disappear gradually and the sun began to shine again. The waves calmed down and everything appeared to be normal like before.

This experience of terror made me realize that life is fragile. Whatever we cling tightly to may disappear or be taken away! At the door of death, I only thought of my family and loved ones. Nothing else was important anymore during the panic moment.

I also realized that God is in control. God gave us life so that we could live eternally. To live eternally, we must learn to trust in God.

To trust in God, we must be humble to follow His will.

To follow His will, we must be obedient to His words.

To be obedient to God's words, we must learn to surrender our hearts to Him.

To surrender our hearts to Him, we must learn to listen to His words.

To listen to God's words, we must learn to pray in faith.

To pray in faith, we must turn off our desire for worldly things.

To turn off our desire for worldly things, we must search our hearts from within.

To search our hearts from within, we must be true and sincere.

To be true and sincere, we must first open our hearts and minds.

To first open our hearts and minds, we must experience joy and contentment.

To experience joy and contentment, we must choose to be happy.

God made us for a purpose.

*"For yesterday is but a dream and tomorrow is just a vision.*
*Today well lived makes every yesterday*
*a dream of happiness*
*and every tomorrow a vision of hope.*
*Look well, therefore, to this day."*

KALIDASA, INDIAN DRAMATIST

*"Life is not measured by the number of breaths we take,*
*but by the number of moments that take our breath away."*

ATTRIBUTION UNKNOWN

## 9

# How to Determine Your Level of Happiness?

This is not a test. Do it in your own sweet time in one sitting. You will discover more about yourself, your strengths, weaknesses and ways to improve in the pursuit of happiness.

On the right, tick whether you agree or disagree with the following situations. Some may not be applicable to you.

| (I) Meaningful Worldly Objects | | | |
|---|---|---|---|
| | Agree | Disagree | N/A |
| 1 I am satisfied with my current housing. | | | |
| 2 I am satisfied with my furnishings in my house. | | | |
| 3 I am satisfied with my wardrobe. | | | |
| 4 I am satisfied with my access to transportation. | | | |
| 5 I am satisfied with my electronic devices (TV, radio, speakers, etc.). | | | |
| 6 I am satisfied with my access to shops where I can find an adequate variety of products. | | | |
| 7 I am satisfied with my car/bike. | | | |
| 8 I am satisfied with my watch, purse/wallet and personal accessories. | | | |

| (II) Money | Agree | Disagree | N/A |
|---|---|---|---|
| 1 I have sufficient money to maintain my desired lifestyle. | | | |
| 2 My level of income and assets are sufficient to secure the respect and perhaps admiration of those people who are important to me. | | | |
| 3 I have enough money to pursue activities that interest me. | | | |
| 4 I can afford to participate in activities that enhance my health and prevent illness. | | | |
| 5 I have sufficient money to obtain quality healthcare when I need it. | | | |
| 6 My level of compensation is fair and reasonable for the work I do. | | | |
| 7 My income and assets are sufficient to provide me with an adequate number of options in everyday living. | | | |
| 8 My income or assets are sufficient to make me feel safe. | | | |
| **(III) Affirmation** | | | |
| 1 I am satisfied with the affirmation I get from people in my community. | | | |
| 2 From co-workers. | | | |
| 3 From my supervisors. | | | |
| 4 From my friends. | | | |
| 5 From my children. | | | |
| 6 From my parents. | | | |
| 7 From my spouse. | | | |
| 8 From God. | | | |

| (IV) Companionship | Agree | Disagree | N/A |
|---|---|---|---|
| 1 I am satisfied with the level of companionship I receive from people in my community. | | | |
| 2 From co-workers. | | | |
| 3 From my friends. | | | |
| 4 From my children. | | | |
| 5 From my parents. | | | |
| 6 From my spouse. | | | |
| 7 From my extended family. | | | |
| 8 Through my relationship with God. | | | |
| (V) Intimacy | | | |
| 1 I am satisfied with the intimacy I have with friends. | | | |
| 2 With my children. | | | |
| 3 With my parents. | | | |
| 4 With my extended family. | | | |
| 5 With my spouse. | | | |
| 6 Within a professional relationship such as pastor, lawyer, or doctor. | | | |
| 7 With a pet. | | | |
| 8 With God. | | | |

| (VI) Health | | | |
|---|---|---|---|
| | Agree | Disagree | N/A |
| 1 I have a general sense of physical well-being. | | | |
| 2 I rarely feel physical pain or discomfort | | | |
| 3 I rarely feel depressed. | | | |
| 4 I rarely feel anxious or worried. | | | |
| 5 I am confident that I will continue to experience physical and emotional well being. | | | |
| 6 I am confident that I will live until 80. | | | |
| 7 I am confident that I won't depend on any medication for the next 20 years. | | | |
| 8 I am confident that I won't depend on any physical help for the next 30 years. | | | |
| (VII) Rewarding Occupation | | | |
| 1 I have mastered the skills required to successfully complete the tasks of my occupation. | | | |
| 2 I enjoy performing the tasks required by my occupation. | | | |
| 3 My job gives me a sense of accomplishment. | | | |
| 4 I like the working hours of my job. | | | |
| 5 I like the traveling time to my workplace. | | | |
| 6 I like the environment of my workplace. | | | |
| 7 I look forward to my job every day. | | | |
| 8 My job enhances my mind to grow. | | | |

| (VIII) Renewing Recreation | Agree | Disagree | N/A |
|---|---|---|---|
| 1 I have sufficient opportunity to engage in activities which have the primary purpose of pleasing me in some way. | | | |
| 2 The recreational activities I choose give me a sense of being refreshed and renewed. | | | |
| 3 I look forward to my recreational activities when I am involved in the task of daily living. | | | |
| 4 I don't mind spending my whole holiday on renewing the recreation which I like. | | | |
| 5 The renewing recreation place is not far from my house. | | | |
| 6 I often join a group of friends in renewing recreation activities. | | | |
| 7 Renewing recreation does not sacrifice my personal time with my family. | | | |
| 8 Renewing recreation does not interfere with my current occupation. | | | |

A SIMPLE GUIDE TO PERSONAL HAPPINESS

| (IX) Freedom | | | |
|---|---|---|---|
| | **Agree** | **Disagree** | **N/A** |
| 1 Any constraints that restrict my actions are reasonable, appropriate and acceptable. | | | |
| 2 I can express my thoughts and feelings without fearing I will be rejected, ridiculed, or punished by people in my community. | | | |
| 3 At work, my speech, decision making and general well being are valued and appreciated. | | | |
| 4 Among friends, I can express my thoughts and feelings without fear I will jeopardize the relationship in some way. | | | |
| 5 With my spouse, I can express my strengths and weaknesses without any fear I will jeopardize the relationship in some way. | | | |
| 6 With my parents, I am free to share my ambitions and aspirations in life. | | | |
| 7 In a shopping mall, I can wander freely without any fear of bumping into any old enemies or old friends. | | | |
| 8 In the park, I can walk, run or jog without fear of being robbed, raped, or murdered. | | | |

| (X) Security | | | |
|---|---|---|---|
| | Agree | Disagree | N/A |
| 1 In the future I will be able to maintain possession of or access to those worldly objects I currently enjoy. | | | |
| 2 In the future I will have enough money to maintain a reasonable, satisfying quality of life. | | | |
| 3 I will be able to maintain interpersonal relationships which provide affirmation. | | | |
| 4 I will be able to maintain interpersonal relationships which provide companionship. | | | |
| 5 I am confident that I will continue to have the degree of health and emotional well being I currently enjoy. | | | |
| 6 In the future I will continue to experience at least the degree of occupational satisfaction I currently enjoy. | | | |
| 7 In the future I will be able to continue at least the degree of enjoyment that my recreational activities currently provide. | | | |
| 8 I am confident future constraints on my actions will be reasonable and appropriate and I will be able to express my thoughts and feelings with members of my community, workplace, family, as well as with friends without fear of jeopardizing those relationships as a result. | | | |

# 10

## Interpreting Your Score

Congratulations! You have successfully completed 80 questions which cover your entire personal life. Remember, this is not a test. The questions were formed to discover your potential, interest and other qualities of life you may be missing.

| Number of "Agree" Answers | Possible Indications |
|---|---|
| 60–80 | You have a very good level of happiness right now. Keep it up and enjoy your life. Help someone today! |
| 40–60 | You are somewhat happy. You can improve your score by applying some of the methods suggested by this book. Press on. |
| 20–40 | You are mostly unhappy with your life. Analyze your perspectives. Do you want to continue living like this or do you want to change for the better, for the sake of your own happiness and the people around you? You can make the change today. |

| 0–20 | Hey! Are you okay? E-mail me and see what I can do for you. Life is not that bad. I suggest you take a long holiday and re-evaluate your needs and wants in your personal life. Do something that you love without worrying about tomorrow too much. My best wishes for you. |

*"No matter how life pushes you down,*
*no matter how much you hurt,*
*you can always bounce back."*
SHERYL SWOOPES

*"If you want to lift yourself up, lift someone else up."*
BOOKER WASHINGTON, TEACHER, AUTHOR

*"The best way to discover yourself*
*is to lose yourself in the service of others."*
GANDHI

A SIMPLE GUIDE TO PERSONAL HAPPINESS

SECTION III

## THE SEARCH FOR HAPPINESS

1

## The Journey Ahead

*"The search for happiness*
*is one of the chief sources for unhappiness."*
ERIC HOFFER

True happiness comes not from material or external factors but from psychological or internal factors. Happiness is a mental, not a physical state, according to some experts. The good news is this means each and every one of us has the potential to be happy. The bad news is your happiness is your own responsibility. You're the only one who can make yourself happy. No one and nothing else can do it for you. Our consumption based economy and perfection obsessed mass culture offers countless keys to happiness.

*"You will never be happy if you continue to search*
*for what happiness consists of.*
*You will never live if you are looking for the meaning of life."*
ALBERT CAMUS

Since happiness is based on internal factors, you need to examine your attitudes toward yourself and your role in the world if you want to find fulfillment.

From the moment we were born, we were taught to be strong, to be smart, to study hard, earn good results in school so that we can get good paying jobs and be rich. Is this the ultimate way to happiness? How come so many wealthy people are not happy?

The more material things they accumulate, the more worries they have. From the history of civilization, we know that money is not the important source of happiness. How we live, how we relate to others, and how many friends we have, bring us true joy and happiness. And yet, very often we ignore our bodies' signals, our senses, our conscience, and our beliefs.

Now is the time to think about our second half of life on this planet. "Do you know where you are going to?" is my favorite song made famous by Diana Ross. The chords' progressions, sweet melody, and powerful lyrics give me fresh directions. Do you have a song which moves you? Pick one today. The Manchester United Football Club has songs to motivate and to unite them. A key speaker from Singapore always loves to sing "A Whole New World" before he starts speaking, which makes him one of the most effective and successful motivational speakers on earth.

To me, happiness is a simple 9 letter word.

H = Heart
A = Say
P = Peace
P = Present
I = Aspiration
N = Nest
E = Existence
S = Soul
S = Song

You must always feel from your *heart, say* what you mean to get the message across and you will find *peace*. Live in your *present*. Don't worry about tomorrow. Forget about the painful past. Live up to your *aspirations*. Build a love *nest* with the people you care about. Rejoice in your *existence*, your place on earth, to make it a better world for everyone especially those who come after us. Help somebody with all your heart, all your *soul*, and all your mind. They will be singing your *song* when you leave someday...

My favorite reminder from the emails I received is; "when

you are born into this world, people all around you smile but you cry, when you leave the world, people all around you cry, and you smile all the way to Heaven." I want to be smiling last. What about you?

Self reflection and acceptance are extremely beneficial and uplifting for the energy in our heart. Awareness and attention are, after all, a way to love yourself. A great amount of peace and relief comes with self-acceptance. Healing and letting go of past hurts will also bring balancing benefits to the present. Letting go of future worries frees up your heart for an enjoyable living now. It is your right to deserve love and acceptance.

> *"It's my experience that you really can't lose*
> *when you try the truth."*
> SHARON STONE

2

## It's All in Your Head

You don't need the best: your best is enough.

Stop looking backward in anger and regret. The past is past.

Stop living in the future: tomorrow is too late.

Don't wait for the best time: there's no time like now, so take action.

Stop being your worst enemy: own your success.

Don't be pessimistic about the future. Things get better.

You have the tools to be happy today. All it takes is changing your attitudes toward yourself and your place in the world.

Don't compare to others. You're just where you're supposed to be.

We confuse pleasure with happiness. The former is sensual and temporary, the latter is spiritual and permanent.

Base decisions on your life, the life you want to lead, not someone else's life or the life others think you should lead. The abandonment of materialism offers freedom.

*"Wealth is like sea-water;*
*the more I drink the thirstier I become."*
ARTHUR SCHOPENHAUER

One of my favorite stories is of a famous Polish rabbi named Hafeg Hayyim. One day a student from far away came to

90

visit him. Upon entering the rabbi's home, the student was surprised to see only books and no furniture in the house. The student asked, "Hi! Rabbi, where is your furniture?" The rabbi answered, "Where is your furniture?" "But Rabbi, I am only a visitor here." To which the rabbi answered, "So am I." the rabbi doesn't have furniture because furniture isn't important to him, even though it is important to others. He has thousands of books, however, because they are important to him. Books, not furniture, give him happiness.

Do you enjoy having a house full of books, as did Rabbi Hayyim? Then by all means, keep stacking them in every corner of your house. Does traveling to Europe every 6 months mean more to you than buying a house like all your friends and associates? Pack your bags. Does being able to see your son's swimming competition mean more to you than becoming President at your firm? Be true to yourself and you'll find you're just where you're supposed to be... and you'll be happy.

Comparing ourselves to others will, little by little, year by year, destroy our chances of happiness in life. It's a race we can never win!

The attitude you need to adopt to ensure that the spark of life remains vibrant, to be happy today, is simple – it gets better. The simple passage of time enhances your life. Keep breathing and your life situation will improve. Time is a sort of river of passing events. I believe time flows through our lives bringing joys, not sorrows, bringing opportunities, not crises. It's a positive force that we can ride to happiness, if only we let ourselves be carried by its currents. You can choose to ride the positive river flowing through your life or you can choose to fight the current and struggle to stay in place.

Time leads to wisdom and happiness, eases pain, lessens anger, and adds perspective. Start taking small, simple, concrete steps in the direction you want and you'll find your attitude changing.

To be happy, you need to own your success. A positive self image will give you the confidence and faith to live life to the fullest. Your personal life, your career, and your finances will all flourish.

Every day before work, I change into walking clothes and go straight to the park. Once I enter the park, the sounds of the city start to grow quiet. After 1 round of walking, the disturbing street noise diminishes, replaced by the sound of my shoes stepping on the pavement and the wind, rustling through the trees. I am focusing on the sound of nature rather than what is annoying me. I am beginning to own my success. I know of people who take up stargazing, others become gardeners, artists or fishermen!

Do you ever find yourself waiting for the perfect moment to make a dreaded telephone call or to tackle a problem assignment? Waiting for the perfect moment means waiting forever. Hesitation delays success, not pain and freezes fear in place. Take action. You'll be happier and spend less time worried and afraid.

Why are we afraid of failing? We've come to think that failing in an action makes us failures as human beings. We assume being a successful person means being perfect. Success, even happiness, is equated with perfection. Yet imperfect is what makes us human.

A holy man was once asked how he could be so sure that he would be welcomed in Heaven. He said that when he stood before the angels, they'd ask him, "Were you always a perfect student?" He'd answer, "No." They asked again, "Were you entirely and completely scrupulous in your prayers and observance?" Again he'd answer, "No." Finally the angels asked, "Were you always charitable and compassionate?" For a third time he'd answer, "No." The angels welcomed him to Heaven because he had spoken the truth. The angels know that no one and nothing is perfect.

Being happy, having a good life that provides emotional, psychological, and spiritual fulfillment and satisfaction means it's impossible to have everything. Sure you can try, but you'll not only be unhappy, you'll probably end up with a migraine from repeatedly banging your head against a wall. Contentment comes when you set priorities and play the hand you've been dealt the best you can. Happiness comes from a well-rounded life.

*"Life is not meant to be fair; it is meant to be life.*
*Therefore it is how we deal with it*
*that makes the difference.*
*It is only when we realize that life is leading us nowhere*
*that it begins to have meaning!"*
P.D. OUSPENSKY, RUSSIAN PHILOSOPHER

*"May you live all the days of your life."*
JONATHAN SWIFT

A SIMPLE GUIDE TO PERSONAL HAPPINESS

3

## Extra Tips

Here is a list of events and situations written down randomly by a few members of the public on a Sunday afternoon. My question to them is, "What makes you happy?"

Sally: The ability to love and to be loved, gratitude and a zest for life.

Melinda: The scent of my son's head, especially after a bath.

John: My baby's big, toothless smile.

Ming: Hearing my teenage sons say, "Love you, Dad," every time we end a phone call.

Elizabeth: An email from Afghanistan.

Suree: Really stopping to savor everyday natural beauty: a surprisingly pink sunrise, wind on the pond, a newly blossomed flower in the garden.

Lance: Brahms Second Symphony.

Alex: Watching a sporting event live. There's so much energy in the crowd.

Linda: A happy sounding dessert if ever there was one.

Tom: Sex! Makes me feel alive from head to toe.

Maslow theorized that we all have 5 types of needs.
  i  Physiological—oxygen, water, food, sleep, sex.
  ii  Safety and security—safe home, job security, savings.
  iii  Love and belonging—marriage, family, friends, community.
  iv  Esteem needs—status, respect, recognition, confidence,

mastery.

v Self-actualization–creativity, beauty, uniqueness, order, self-sufficiency, meaningfulness.

Maslow believed that people addressed their needs in this order. In other words, you wouldn't seek to meet your esteem needs until you have addressed your love and belonging needs. Setting aside the validity of his other ideas, what's important for us is that Maslow divided human needs into distinct categories. Rather than look to one aspect of your life to meet all or even most of your needs, expand your reach. Give time and energy to the varied aspects of your life that you know will give you the best opportunity to meet your different needs.

To achieve contentment, we need to make compromises and choices. Nothing is certain in life, but generally the chances of happiness are greater if one has multiple areas of interests and involvement. To juggle is to diminish the risk of depression, anxiety and sadness. You can do anything but not everything. The universe is full of creative projects that are waiting to be done. So, if you really care about quality of life, if you want to relax, don't focus on materialism. Control your aspirations. That will simplify things. That will also lead to happiness.

Think of these choices as addition by subtraction. You're adding to your happiness by giving up the drive to be the best at everything. Figure out all the values which are important to you and do the best you can in each. You can't give 100 percent effort to anything, unless there's nothing else in your life. It's fine to give 40 percent to your insurance career, 50 percent effort to your family and 10 percent to playing the guitar. These are not sacrifices. The only thing you'll be losing is your frustration.

Forgiveness is a gift. It's not a gift for the person who transgressed against you, it's a gift for you. Forgiving allows you to put the past behind you. It lets you stop being a victim. Forgiveness is empowering. In the Bible, Peter asks Jesus how many times he has to forgive his brother if he keeps wronging him, suggesting 7 times should be sufficient. Jesus responds by saying 7 isn't nearly enough;

instead Peter should plan on forgiving his brother 70 times 7 times. In other words, there's no limit to how many times someone should be forgiven. Human betterment is a gradual, two steps forward, one step back effort. Forgive others for their misdeeds over and over and over again. This gesture fosters inner ease. Forgive yourself over and over and over again. Stop living in the past and you can embrace the image of yourself as an empowered individual, an individual who finds happiness in this multi cultural and complex world.

Happiness is a state of mind, not a goal. The life you want is here, now waiting for you to grab it. Too many of us spend our lives planning and hoping and dreaming about how wonderful life could be tomorrow if we got a promotion, strike it rich on a lottery, bought our dream car, dream house. We say that we will be happy when we lose 30 pounds, get our salary up to $100,000 a year, our kids go to the ivy league universities, or we pay off our mortgage and credit card bills.

Always too eager for the future, we pick up bad habits of expectancy. We act as if happiness relies on other people, on fate, or on forces beyond our control. As a result, we fail to see how wonderful our lives are today. Pin your hopes on the future, you'll miss your chance. Take responsibility for your own happiness, and start living today. Tomorrow is too late.

If you try to look so hard to the future for happiness, you will indeed always have the possibility of achieving contentment but you'll never actually get there. It's as if you're on a voyage looking for the edge of the earth. You keep traveling, thinking the edge of the earth is right there at the horizon line. But no matter how long you travel, how far you go, you never actually get there. Your goal is always visible but always out of reach. Live your life this way, rely on the future for your happiness, you're a human becoming, not a human being.

Only God knows what the future holds, so your counting on the future to provide the environment that will finally make you happy isn't just foolish, it's presumptuous. Stop writing the script for tomorrow. Today is not just a dress rehearsal, it's your actual living...

*"If there is no wind, row."*
LATIN PROVERB

*"We either make ourselves miserable
or we make ourselves strong.
The amount of work is the same."*
CARLOS CASTANEDA

4

# Enough is Abundance

The need to own and to consume more and more "things" seems finally to be leaving many of us cold and empty. Many have begun looking within ourselves for a vision that will sustain our deepest longings. How much or how little do we need to be happy? In his book, "Man's Search for Himself," Rollo May wrote that "knowing what one wants and the ability to choose one's own values. Happiness itself depends not on property but on expression. When we experience life in all its dimensions—sensual, spiritual, and practical, we begin to see that much of what we want and think we need in order to live a good life is unnecessary, we are relieved to find that we can be happy with what we have."

The 19th century poet William Wordsworth saw even in his time, the price we pay for buying our way to happiness: "the world is too much with us, late and soon, getting and spending, we lay waste to our powers; little we see in nature that is ours, we have given our hearts away, a sordid boon!"

We can reclaim our hearts and live more graciously in the modern world by re-awakening our senses to everything around us. Through our senses, we draw our experience of what it means to be alive. In observing nature, we observe the essence of living. We are our senses. Whenever we open our eyes, our hearts, and our minds, we can expand our senses of discovery, of wonder, and of pleasure—our own aliveness to life.

*"Enough is abundance to the wise."*
EURIPIDES

*"The great and glorious masterpiece of men*
*is to live to the point."*
MICHEL DE MONTAIGNE

*"To lead a simple life in reasonable comfort,*
*with a minimum of possessions,*
*ranks high among the arts of living.*
*It leaves us time, resources, and freedom of mind we need*
*for the things that give life value;*
*LOVING, HELPING, SERVING and GIVING."*
EKNATH EASWARAN

*"The peace of mind that you're looking for*
*is present all the time."*
JOAN BORYSENKO

*'Friends, books, a cheerful heart, and conscience clear,*
*are the most choice companions we have here."*
WILLIAM MATHER

We pay for "new and improved." We have increased our standard of living and now must work hard to maintain it, leaving little time to enjoy what we have. In addition to time poverty, we feel doomed never to have enough money to support our lives.

When we stop and explore what makes life rich and fulfilling we find the answer not in all our accumulated possessions, but in our simple ability to take pleasure in the moment, in what is around us, free for taking! We have been overworking for things we don't really need, chasing technology in hot haste. We have become more mechanical and less spiritual. On its own, no amount of technical development can lead to lasting happiness.

When we're not in a constant state of haste, all our senses become more alert and our potential to enjoy life is expanded immeasurably. We live more graciously in the modern world by re-awakening, and it is in this state that we truly find ourselves. When we slow down, we can live more fully in the moment and more deeply within ourselves. Wherever we are, we can even slow down enough to reveal passions we never knew we had.

When we are happy or sad, whether we feel blessed or lost, whether we feel lightness of being or the heaviness of pain, what's important, ultimately, what makes us feel most alive is our alertness to the richness of experience. When we savor this desire for awakening as a hope and a possibility, we can always feed our souls and make contact with our inner life. This is what makes life precious.

I live for the possibilities of the moment. I don't neglect the broad picture of life, the needs of others, or a sense of my larger responsibilities. I am always alert to snap up those illuminating moments when I feel open to all the rhythms of life.

*"Thinking a smile all the time will keep your face youthful."*
FRANK BURGERS

*"I never had to go anywhere to find my paradise."*
EMILY DICKINSON

*"When you have only two pennies left in the world, buy a loaf of bread with one, and a lily with the other."*
CHINESE PROVERB

5

# Tale of 3 Countries

### i The Rembrandt Connection

In 1999, I spent winter in Amsterdam. It was cold, wet and windy. Everyone was talking about Y2K, the year 2000, when computers might break or create havoc in all the systems of the electronic world! Well! Nothing happened and life goes on...

In Amsterdam, I visited Rembrandt's Museum which was his actual final house in Holland. I learned about this great master artist in 1987 when I took 2 semesters of Art History Survey at the College of Fine and Professional Arts in Kent State University, Ohio, USA.

Most of Rembrandt's collections and gifts were still there on the shelves in his 3 storey home. I began to understand why he painted the great sea-shell, the soldier's helmet, the Chinese spear and some of the most beautiful table cloths on earth.

When I stepped into his drawing chamber, I paused, took a deep breath, closed my eyes and began to imagine Rembrandt, sitting down crafting and drawing with his unique tools. I could feel his presence in the entire house. The sense of history, the timelessness of human pleasure, our connectedness to each other, nourished and sustained by our senses, filled me with awe that day and held me in a timeless embrace.

Modern technology and advances in the forms and varieties of entertainment cannot match the richness of our own sensory experience. The gifts of daily life are the simple things that surround us. When we pay close attention to these, we discover the magical inner life of all things we encounter everyday.

Our homes are places we can express and enjoy many pleasures. Here we can be free and creative. Our home is a canvass on which we paint many things—still lifes, landscapes, portraits, anything that moves us in a deeply personal way. Our ability to experience, to be fully open to life through our hearts and our senses is within our control.

## ii A Passion for Ducks

One of my favorite pastimes is to watch ducks swimming or walking to find food. A more perfect scenario is when a mother ducks leads 5 or 6 other ducklings. In the water they seem to swim effortlessly and tirelessly, creating little wave lines as they glide in curvy patterns. When they are tired, they sit down on the ground and hide part or all of their heads into their bodies, so peaceful and calm.

I am not alone in my passion for ducks. In Minoru Park during spring time in Vancouver, all kinds or people, young and old, whites and Asians, blacks and Hispanics, all stop to have a good look at these gentle creatures, which can fly, swim, walk, and run! This is one sure way I know, to restore peacefulness and tranquility to my life–watching nature takes place, right in front of my eyes.

## iii A Friend from Ecuador

When I was working in New York in the early nineties, I met an artist from Ecuador who earned his living driving the yellow cab–New York's most famous taxi company.

Boris loved to paint when he was drunk! He told me that when he was drunk, his mind felt free and he painted whatever he wanted, often creating some of his greatest masterpieces while listening to the music of Bob Dylan, his favorite singer.

Boris has shown me his secrets of happiness–to indulge in his passions while he is not driving the taxi, without any fear of rejection, without anyone telling him what to paint. Living in New York City is Boris's dream come true. He told me that he had a son and a daughter back in the mountains of Ecuador and he regularly sent gifts home to them. Knowing Boris has made me realize that again and again, happiness lies in your hands and no one can take happiness away from us. He has also introduced me to Lin Yutang.

*"Perhaps the best way to thank God for the gift of living*
*is to appreciate the present hour,*
*to sit quietly and hear your own breathing,*
*and look out on the universe and be content."*
LIN YUTANG

Having lived in Vancouver for several months now convinced me that, to experience the joy of living, it is essential to take time being alone. The space of time and distance from home have allowed me to become more conscious of what I have control over and what I don't. I am awakened to what really matters and guided to look beyond temporary distractions and annoyances in order to carry out my planned intentions. I am in a good place, free to be fully myself. I also learned to avoid negative distractions by letting them enter me and float away, without becoming overly disturbed by anything.

You will need to make a commitment to quiet time. Try to acquire the habit of checking in with yourself. Several times a day just take a minute and ask yourself how you are feeling. Listen to your own answer. Respond kindly. If you are working very hard, promise yourself a break and treat afterward. Any good thought you have is a prayer.

*"Silence is the perfectest herald of joy.*
*I were but little happy if I could say how much."*
WILLIAM SHAKESPEARE

*"True happiness is a of retired nature*
*and an enemy to pomp and noise,*
*it arises, in the first place, from the enjoyment of one's self,*
*and in the next, from friendship and conversations*
*of a few select companions."*
JOSEPH ADDISON

6

## More Extra Tips

### i Letting Go

One of life's biggest challenges is the challenge of letting go. On an intellectual level I am certain you can understand and appreciate what I am referring to, each of us has been created with a built-in mechanism that wants us to maintain the status quo. Despite how much we want a better life, we do tend to stick with what we know to be safe and comfortable. Keeping things the same, even if your life situation is awful, is safe compared with abandoning what you have and facing the unknown.

The unknown is where all of your personal and professional potential lies. The known, on the other hand, is the life you are living right now. Keep things as they are and resent being limited, or opt for the discomfort of change as you face the unknown. As long as these choices are just about the only two choices available to you, you get to choose your destiny. Choose sameness and you get more of what you have. Choose change and letting go, and a whole new world of possibilities awaits you.

You will grow when you let go. Improving the quality of your life takes work, maximize the positive moments of each day of your life. There is always a trade off. Take stock of every single thing that holds you back and exchange these limitations for a life of limitless potential, a life that is more personally and professionally rewarding.

### ii Dash of Life

The better you make yourself, the better you make every area of your personal and professional life and everyone with whom you come into contact.

The more you elevate your standards of personal excellence, the more you will notice that the other people in your sphere of influence raise their standards. Letting go of the past demands determination, and if you really are intent on improving your life, you are going to have to make some bold changes.

To improve your dash is to increase your level of information. You begin the moment you decide to increase your level of personal happiness. Deciding to enjoy the moments of your life and be happier is what a more fulfilling dash of life is all about.

Happy people tend to be grateful for what they have and are non-judgmental of others. Give up judging other people and decide to be happy today.

### iii Increase Your Resourcefulness

Hard work makes dreams come true, and a great work ethic can be one of your greatest assets as you build a better future for yourself. By dedicating yourself totally to being more creative and resourceful, you will pave the way for a life that is more fulfilling as well as more fun. Resourceful people have incredibly high levels of focused energy. They do not function by the clock, rather they define their days by the accomplishment of their projects.

They are willing to get up early and sleep late to change their lives. In this very instant, you can decide to increase your levels of personal urgency and resourcefulness and make things happen in your life, instead of waiting for things to happen to you.

Control your thoughts for they will become your words.
Control your words for they will become your actions.
Control your actions for they will become your habits.
Control your habits for they will become your character.

Control your character for they will become your destiny.

When you choose to change your life for the greater good, what's in the best interest of yourself and others, your life takes on greater meaning and the achievements of your life become more worthwhile.

There is a very big difference between motivation and willpower. Motivation tends to come from an outside source and it is very often short in duration. I have never seen a person who relied on motivation accomplish long term success in his or her life. However, the people I know that have the internal drive created by sheer willpower seem to be able to work miracles.

They function with great clarity about their goals, certain about achieving those goals, and they continually move in the direction of their desires. Willpower comes from passion, and when you are passionate about something you will be inspired to greatness. Our minds work in pictures, not in words. Our words create images in our minds and when we lock on to those images, what we envision can become our reality. When you engage and direct your vivid imagination toward what you want, you change your world!

### iv Willing to be Coached

Very few people have the capacity to change their lives dramatically and permanently by themselves. If you are willing to admit that you need some help and support in transforming your life, find a coach.

Comfort in life is fine unless it prevents us from moving forward and we become bogged down in a rut. Human nature causes us to go with what we know, both in situations and relationships. It's that thirst for safety, security and sameness that very often causes us to settle into a life that is habitual rather than stimulating and exciting. When that happens, our tendency is to stop finding our own happiness. That's when you need a coach to tell you what to do, show you how to do it, and hold you personally accountable for the completion of your tasks. A great coach is a mentor who creates a system that keeps you moving in the direction of what you have mutually agreed to accomplish.

### v Make Happiness Your Destiny

We can never know what the future holds in store for us, and we may never understand how we arrived at the present condition. What we do know is that our destiny will largely be driven by our beliefs and behaviors.

Armed with this information, we can consciously make better choices in our lives. As a result of these choices, we can increase the likelihood of finding and achieving our destiny. When you deliberately seek opportunities to advance your life, these opportunities will appear.

Seize these opportunities and make the most of them. When you do, you are on your way to enjoy the happiness you desire and so richly deserve. Find your passion once again and miracles can occur in your lifetime.

### vi Future Vision

We become what we think most of the time and the things that we focus on are likely to become our destiny. Thoughts are things, and thoughts have power and energy. So, be mindful of your thoughts and prayers because what you think and pray for will come true!

A good question to ask yourself when it comes to your future is, "If I were not living my present life, what would my new life look like?"

Write down precisely what your new life looks like and focus on that image on a daily basis. Wonderful things will happen to and for you as your future begins to reflect the things you focus your mental energy on.

The best way to change tomorrow is to take care of today.

### vii Too Busy?

Many of us are simply too busy to find a moment for our dreams. When you have too much to do, finding time to get involved in activities you love isn't an option. Even when you do have time, you can't remember how to use it for yourself. Add kids to the equation and you've got a life with no free time at all.

Feeling hurried and harried isn't entirely the result of having so much to do. Many people do just as much in a

A SIMPLE GUIDE TO PERSONAL HAPPINESS

state of calmness. When you're too rushed to think clearly, you lose any sense of what doesn't have to be done and pile on more work than necessary. You need even more down-time when you're constantly in a state of controlled alarm, because you're not nourished by what you're doing–you're drained by it.

Overworked people are scared. They're scared of forgetting to do something, or not meeting a deadline, or letting someone down. They're scared of being overwhelmed by things out of control. That's why they never think to make their lives easier or more fun; they just add on more responsibilities.

You need to throw yourself heart and soul into something you love and give it your very best effort. You need to push past your boredom barriers and take at least one of your passions to the absolute limit you're capable of. You will never be happy if you don't choose something to which you can give your very best. Pick something that you're enthused about, some thing you'd like to share with the world. Think of this project you want to leave behind when you go.

Don't worry about it too much. Your first attempts at accomplishing something might be valuable only because they teach you about yourself and how you work. You might not finish them at all. You have to learn how to throw your heart into something you love and not ask for it back until you have something to present to the world. Pick something that appeals to you and wholeheartedly throw yourself into it. Hold nothing back. Complete a book, produce a play, build a computer, pass an exam, or set up your house as an art gallery and schedule an open house for your own paintings.

You can only achieve your best if you do everything you love. To be truly happy, you must learn to do everything you love or not anything at all! Live your life on your own terms, do everything you love, freely, with passion, purpose, and real results!

*"There are 2 things to aim for in life:*
*first, to get what you want;*
*and second, to enjoy it.*

*Many achieve the first,*
*but only the wisest achieve the second."*
LOGAN SMITH, AUTHOR

*"It is not a miracle that we do this work.*
*The miracle is that we enjoy it."*
MOTHER TERESA

7

## Bruce Lee and Albert Einstein

Bruce Lee and Albert Einstein are still two of the most well known men in this century. Both have lived their own distinctive lives and left a mark in the history of human civilization.

Bruce Lee once said, "I have come to understand that life is best to be lived and not to be conceptualized. I am happy because I am growing daily and I am honestly not knowing where the limit lies."

There are 2 kinds of happiness in this world. The one most of us think of is simply feeling wonderful in your body. The other is a state of being in perfect harmony with life and the universe. This is the state psychologists call "flow," musicians call "the groove," and athletes call "the zone."

When you eat your favorite food or do activities that you like, you have a natural endorphin release to make you feel good. According to medical research, endorphins are neuro-transmitters, they create more bonding in the brain, so every time you experience an endorphin release, it actually makes you more intelligent. Every cell in your body has receptors for endorphins. Not only can every cell in our body experience happiness, but the more often we choose to be happy, the more intelligent we become!

Here are 8 happiness triggers—

i Clear goals.
   ii Immediate feedback.
  iii Ability to concentrate on the task at hand.
  iv The possibility of successful completion.
   v Total involvement.
  vi Loss of self consciousness.
 vii A sense of control.
viii Time distortion.

By taking control over even the simplest elements of our environment such as where we sit, how books are arranged on our desk, or even what we are looking at when we day-dream, we increase the likelihood of experiencing happiness in our every day lives.

Time distortion is when minutes become hours and hours feel like minutes.

Here are 8 time distortion activities—
    i Sports that test your ability.
   ii Reading an interesting book.
  iii Going for a massage.
  iv Noticing the subtle difference in taste of different curry restaurants.
   v Watching a favorite movie with your loved ones.
  vi Going on holiday in a foreign country.
 vii Listening to a Mozart symphony.
viii Playing kite with your kids.

Albert Einstein once said, "Put your hand on a hot stove for a minute, it seems like an hour. Sit with a pretty girl for an hour, it seems like a minute. That's relativity."

Most of us have at least occasionally experienced the calm, focused energy that comes with performing in the flow zone, when we feel up to the challenges we are faced with. Life, at its best, is a constant shuttle between mastery and challenge, a continual process of stretching and consolidating our gains and learning.

How do we design and adjust our experience to ensure we have the highest possible chance of both enjoying an activity and performing at our best? The key is in the word perception–that is, by adjusting our perceptions (of the challenges we face and of our ability to meet those challenges), we can recreate our experience for optimal performance.

J.M. Barrie said, "The secret of being happy is not doing what one likes, but liking what one does." Pleasure gives the body pleasant sensations; satisfaction gratifies the soul. A lizard will starve to death if you try to hand feed it, yet it will thrive when allowed to hunt its own food. An ear of corn will rot on the stalk if not challenged by wind or rain.

If you want to be happy, you need to take on a worthy challenge, even if that's the last thing you feel you want.

Here are 3 suggestions to create a happier, more satisfying life—

i   Allow more enjoyment into your life
    It is okay to take time out to listen to the rain, take a warm, candlelit bath, watch football in action on a big screen TV, look at the birds in the sky, attend to some flowers, bathe your dog, cut your daughter's fingernails, hug your teenage son, or just close your eyes and relax.

ii  Discover your strong points and begin to put them to work
    We tend to feel our best when we are doing our best, and we can only do our best when we are doing what we do best. While conventional wisdom encourages us to develop our weaknesses, research into success and fulfillment points out that when we play to our strengths and manage our weaknesses, we not only perform better, but we get more satisfaction from our performance.

iii Do at least one difficult thing each day
    Every day the happy person does at least one difficult thing. While it may seem odd to share a lesson in happiness by talking about deliberately seeking out difficulties; it is a lesson that life itself continually attempts to teach us. When seeking out worthy challenges in your own life, bear in mind that optimal experience tends to live at the balancing point at the outer edge of your abilities when you are fully engaged but not overwhelmed by the challenge.

An optimist and a pessimist will both ultimately arrive at the same dreary destination. But the optimist always wins, because he has enjoyed the journey.

I am sure both Bruce Lee and Albert Einstein enjoyed their journeys on earth. They left behind not only their names, but respect and inspiration that have changed the world since they left the world.

8

## Reaching Out to Others

Although we need solitude to gather ourselves after the push and pull of our busy lives, our solitude would be a lonely place if it didn't lead us out of ourselves toward the love and company of other people. Be they friends, family or co-workers, other people play an important part in our lives.

Peter Brown said that," Celebration is the recognition of a moment of joy." We cannot celebrate alone. Celebration needs company of friends, family and relatives, the more the merrier.

Marcel Proust reminded us to, "Let us be grateful to people who make us happy; they are the charming gardeners who make our souls blossom." People who make us happy can be near or far away. Always remember the glow in the faces, their smiles, their kind hearts and their love.

*"A good laugh and a long sleep are the best two cures."*
IRISH PROVERB

*"Happiness is like perfume,*
*you can't pour it on somebody else*
*without getting a few drops on yourself."*
JAMES VAN DER ZEE

*"We know nothing of tomorrow;*
*our business is to be good and happy today."*
SYDNEY SMITH

9

## Passport to a New Perspective

I always know where my passport is. I reach for it whenever my wanderlust beckons. Time spent in new surroundings, whether near or far, gives us a fresh perspective on life. Just as we step back a few feet in order to see Monet's painting of "Water Lilies" more clearly, when we take a few steps onto distant soil, our lives can become a little clearer too.

When we get away, new vistas open up to us just when we think we've seen them all. If you live in a city, go to the country. If you live in the country, go to the city. The more different the place, the better. Widen your path, deepen your understanding, expand your interests and expose yourself to new passions.

Traveling teaches us to accept that some things are out of our hands. We miss the plane and have to wait for another. In 1998, I was flying from Los Angeles, California, to Cleveland, Ohio. The snow storm forced the plane to land in Denver, Colorado. After being stranded for more than 8 hours at the Denver Airport, the airline decided to put us up for the night. I got a free trip to witness the majestic Rocky Mountains and the cool snow village. To me, the delay was a gift and a good night's sleep after about 14 hours of flight from Taiwan. The whole adventure widened my path, expanded my interest, and imparted important lessons about life and myself.

Travel teaches us that people perform similar rituals in different, diverse ways. They worship differently, their cuisine, architecture, way of dressing, and socializing are unique, giving the particular space a rich history, tradition and spirit.

I enjoy my trips from the minute I begin to plan them, by reading about my destination and deciding where to stay. I find it all thrilling, including the wait in the train.

In the spring of 2005, I was on a one way ticket from Zurich, Switzerland, to Vienna, Austria, on a long train journey which went through the magnificent French, Swiss, and the Austrian Alps. The whole journey was like a dream come true: lakes, mountains, little cottages, centuries old towns and passengers up and down, captivated my senses, as the train stopped to pick up passengers from around 100 stations between the two cities.

As a result of an accident involving a van on the railway tracks, I was stranded for half a day in the middle of the Alps. It was cold and dark and I ran out of snacks. Initially I was planning to have my first dinner in Vienna. It looked like I had to wait to have breakfast then. We had not even reached Salzburg, the birthplace of Mozart.

Sitting opposite me was a doctor from Iran, on my right hand side was a tour agent from France and on my left side, a local Austrian girl waiting impatiently to meet up with her boyfriend in Vienna. We all looked different but our needs were the same. We were really hungry and tired but were happy as we got to know each other.

The everyday things that I take for granted in my daily life become a source of fascination when I travel. I see how people put their mark in the world by the specific ways they respond to the challenges and mysteries of life.

I've seen how people eat in Frankfurt, Germany, how they transport themselves in Macau, China, what people wear in Paris, France, how they talk to each other in Bangkok, Thailand, how they roller blade in Singapore, how they dance in New York and how they rush in Tokyo, Japan. Each trip has helped train me to be more discerning and more aware of the intriguing nuances of everyday life.

Traveling is a feast for the senses too. Everywhere I turn, I can see, smell, touch, hear and taste a new world. The lights in Hong Kong, the colors of the northern lights in Canada,, the noise of a basketball match in Madison Square, the taste of delicious curry in Indonesia, and the smoky smell of the streets of Kuala Lumpur, all open me to new heights of appreciation for the sensory rich world around us.

I've participated in grand, colorful street fairs and parades, bursting with life and celebration in London. I love the crowded streets of Zhuhai, where the energy is intense. I also enjoy going to the American flea markets looking at antiques. Going to the New Ming Yuan Palace allowed me to visualize the past glory of the Chinese Emperors who lived there. Experiencing Wales to explore the ruins of the many castles was an incredible adventure. Seeing the world in one day at the "Windows of the World" in Shenzhen really amazed me!

Jon Kabat-Zinn said, "You must be willing to let life itself become your teacher." Each travel experience has a way of opening up to absorb even of the life that surrounds us. We are drawn to places where we forget ourselves and become awestruck, spellbound, lost in a boundless, ever regenerating astonishment at how truly marvelous the world is. All we have to do is show up and be there in a state of appreciation, and happiness will follow.

Life is an ongoing process. You can never tell. Every moment has the potential for meaning. Perhaps all any of us can learn, so that our lives are changed, is what we learn from our own personal experience. As we accept more of life, become more open to ourselves and learn to trust our deepest selves more, we come to trust life more and find happiness and joy along the way.

*"One of the pleasantest things in the world is the journey."*
WILLIAM HAZLITT

*"He who makes time precious, lives forever."*
PETER BROWN

*"Every day is a little life*
*and our whole life is but a day repeated.*
*Therefore, live every day as if it would be the last."*
JOSEPH HALL

## 10

## Before I Say Goodbye

It has been an enjoyable journey writing and compiling facts and information of my personal life for your reading pleasure. My final sharing to you is always live up to your personal potential in whatever you do. Please don't interpret this advice as constant pressure to always be an achiever. See it more in a long term context of pursuing the happy life that you have always dreamed about. Remember you are not alone in your journey. Dean Barrett in his book, "Searching for the Peach Blossom Spring" has really inspired me in pursuing happiness. I am now convinced I am not the only person in this world to want to break free, soaring high like an eagle.

Invest both time and money to learn how to remove the obstacles to your personal happiness and replace them with happiness opportunities. The return on this investment would be enormous. In the end, this is really what it is all about. "Joy to the world!"

*"Happiness is the whole aim and end of human existence."*
ARISTOTLE

*"For I know the plans I have for you, declares the Lord.*
*Plans to prosper you and not harm you,*
*plans to give you hope and a future."*
JEREMIAH 29:11

Would you rather have money or be rich? To have money, you can buy anything you want. Money brings a certain level of happiness and affords you freedom to travel and to give freely. To be rich from the inside, you can start to live your best life now. You don't have to wait for the stock market to rise or be concerned about your investment and returns.

Spread your love and share your happiness to the world. This is the real meaning of being rich.

Once I met two men in the swimming pool, one older and one younger. The older man told me he was 50 and his son 24, was diligently running his family business. I said, "Wow! You look like 40!" He was even more happy and shared all his secrets of happiness with me for the next 2 hours. I learned so much from him that day.

Now it's time for this book to end, and for your future to begin. Personal happiness is within your reach. I wish you joy, abundance, good health and happiness of all kinds.

**Notes**

KC FOONG

# Notes

A SIMPLE GUIDE TO PERSONAL HAPPINESS

**Notes**

KC FOONG

# Notes

Appendix A

# 11 Qualities of Happiness

1  **Love**—This is the wellspring of happiness, renewable and everlasting. We often think that being loved is the best feeling in the world, but it's second best. The best is loving someone else. Love is the opposite of fear. It is the antidote to fear and the first step toward happiness.

2  **Optimism**—Optimism provides power over painful events. I used to think it was an attitude: seeing a glass half full instead of half empty. But that felt artificial, a mere trick or perception. Then I suffered the worst event of my life. My father died. I thought the light had left my life forever. In my deepest despair, I realized that my father had left me a legacy of love that was mine forever, and that if I could survive the loss of my father, nothing else could devastate me. When I realized this, I found that every hurtful event holds lessons and that the more it hurts, the more I learn.

3  **Courage**—This is your strongest weapon for overcoming the split second power of the fear system. We can't rise above fear without courage. If fear is eternally programmed into our brains, so is courage. It is the product of the spirit, the intellect and the higher emotions of love and generosity. It is nature's natural balance

for the fear that has helped us survive. It's a quality that allows us to thrive.

4 **Humor**—Humor is a shift of perception that gives people the guts to go on when life looks its worst. It lifts suffering off the heart and hands it to the intellect and spirit, which alone have the power to heal it.

5 **Health**—Happiness and health are interdependent. It's hard to be happy if you don't feel healthy, and it's hard to be healthy if you're not happy. Of special importance for happiness is healthy mood chemistry. You can have a happy life and not even know it if you're tortured by faulty mood chemistry.

6 **Spirituality**—Happy people aren't afraid to go beyond the boundaries of their own lives. They let go, and welcome extraordinary experiences. They have markedly less fear of death. They're not concerned about dying–they're concerned about not living.

7 **Freedom**—Nothing fills the soul like freedom. Freedom is choice and the choice is what makes us human. When we choose, we define who we are. Everyone has the power to make choices but unhappy people don't know they have it. They think it's only for the rich. Choice is available to anyone who has courage to exercise it.

8 **Proactivity**—Happy people participate in their own destinies and forge their own happiness. They don't wait for events or other people to make them happy. They're not passive victims.

9 **Security**—Happy people know that nothing, over time, lasts–not money, not approval, not even life itself. So, they don't measure security with a calendar or a calculator. They simply like who they are. They're not slaves to popularity, longevity, or financial status. They know that security is an inside job.

10 **Perspective**—Unhappy people tend to see things in absolute terms and often can't distinguish small problems from big ones. Happy people see shades of gray,

and they know how to prioritize their problems and turn them into possibilities. They don't lose sight of life's big picture during bad times.

11 **Purpose**—Happy people know why they're here on earth. They're doing the things they were meant to do. If they died today, they would be satisfied with their lives.

Appendix B

## 6 Happiness Tools

1  **Appreciation**—Appreciation is the purest, strongest form of love. It is the outward-bound kind of love that asks for nothing and gives everything.

2  **Choice**—Choice is the father of freedom and the voice of the heart. Having no choice or options leads to depression, anxiety and the condition called learned helplessness. Choice can govern perception. Happy people choose the course of their lives. Unhappy people make the mistake of giving into the automatic fear reaction which limits their choices drastically, to just fighting, fleeing, or freezing. Happy people turn away from fear and find that intellect and spirit contain a vast warehouse of choices.

3  **Personal Power**—Personal power has two components: taking responsibility and taking action. It means realizing that your life belongs to you and you alone. Personal power keeps you from being a victim. When your personal power is at its peak, you're secure. You don't need to be popular, be right, and have money in the bank. You can handle whatever life dishes out.

4  **Leading with Your Strength**—When you give in to the automatic fear reaction, it makes you focus on your

weaknesses. But when you take the path of the intellect and spirit, you naturally begin to focus on your strength. People often think that fixing their weaknesses will save them but it rarely works. It's just too painful. Leading with your strengths feels good, and that's why it works.

5 **The Power of Language and Stories**—We don't describe the world we see–we see the world we describe. Language, as the simple most fundamental force of the human intellect, has the power to alter perception. We think in words and these words have the power to limit us or to set us free. They can frighten us or evoke our courage. Similarly, the stories we tell ourselves about our own lives eventually become our lives. We can tell healthy stories or horror stories. The choice is ours.

6 **Multidimensional Living**—There are 3 primary components of life: relationships, health and purpose (which is usually work). Many people put all their energy into one area. The most common choice is work, because work best assures us of our survival. Other people become obsessed with relationships (love), and some people limit their lives in the name of longevity. None of this works. Happiness comes from a full life.

Appendix C

## 5 Happiness Traps

**First Trap**—Almost nobody thinks they have enough. Materialism is not making our society happier. It's making us miserable. All too often, people become financially successful by just following money, engaging in high paying jobs they don't really like. Happy people choose their jobs–they follow their passions. When most people talk about leisure they're really talking about the relaxation and sense of freedom that comes from being free from worry–qualities happy people almost always have, even though they're busy.

Social status is alluring and is also a slippery slope. No matter how high you climb, there are countless people still above you. Feeling superior to others is always tempting, but it's a terribly weak tool for achieving happiness. It may pamper your self image but it will never bring you peace of mind. Happy people get their status from within. Their status symbols are things like a happy family, good friends, and pride in their work.

| Happiness and Income in Economically Advanced Nations. | | |
|---|---|---|
| Nations | Happiness Ranking | Income Index |
| Switzerland | 1st | 4th |
| Denmark | 2nd | 19th |

| Canada | 3rd | 16th |
| Ireland | 4th | 48th |
| Netherlands | 5th | 24th |
| United States | 6th | 1st |
| Finland | 7th | 31st |

Financial security is not a path to happiness. We age, we become ill, we lose people we love, we die. Happy people have the courage to embrace their insecurity. They know it will always be there–as long as mankind is mortal–and that to experience it is to feel the true, rough essence of real life.

If you adopt arrangement of your own life as a primary goal, you'll be able to participate in your own destiny. But if you spend your energy struggling for complete control, you'll lose the reins of management and become another leaf in the wind: participation in your own destiny can help make you happy, but struggling for power cannot. Unfortunately, millions of people toil their whole lives away in the pursuit of power, perfectionism, control, status and possessions. There's a word for these people: unhappy.

**Second Trap**—Among happy people today, pleasure is reserved for celebration, to celebrate small achievements such as finishing a day's work. They celebrate more important occasions such as holidays and family members' birthdays.

Unhappy people stay too long at the party and end up celebrating celebrations. They fall into a lifeless trance and indulge robotically, losing track of what they're doing to their bodies. For a short time they're free from fear. When they return to normal life the next morning, they're saddled with guilt, toxicity, and heightened physical addiction. This is a big price to pay for a happiness strategy that doesn't work!

**Third Trap**—Trying to be happy by resolving the past.

**Fourth Trap**—Trying to be happy by overcoming weaknesses.

**Fifth Trap**—Trying to force happiness.

Appendix D

## 10 Defining Moments

1 Where are you at this moment?

2 How old are you and what do you like?

3 Who is there with you, or who is supposed to be there with you?

4 What is happening that makes this moment so significant?

5 What emotions or changes of emotions are you experiencing at this time? Loneliness? Anger? Fear? Confusion? Joy? Power? Helplessness?

6 How would you change this situation if you could?

7 What is your mental/physical experience? Are you in a mental fog or are you clear minded? What do you smell? Taste? Feel? Are you happy or sad? Are you in pain? Weak? Paralyzed?

8 If you could speak to someone now, who would it be? What would you say?

9 What are you saying to yourself?

10 What do you need right now more than anything else?

Appendix E

## Your 7 Critical Choices

Based on these 8 areas of your life;
  Personal Life — Physical Life
  Professional Life — Family
  Education — Spiritual Fulfillment
  Social Life — Relationships

Answer these 7 questions in each of the areas above.
  1  What was the choice?

  2  Why did you make it?

  3  What alternatives did you give up by making this choice?

  4  Where were you, in terms of your self concept, immediately before this choice, and what was your self concept after this choice?

  5  Write a paragraph to describe the long term residual effect of that critical choice.

  6  Write down how and why you think the critical choice either clarified or distorted your authentic self.

  7  Review your interpretation of and reaction to the critical choice. Decide whether or not you believe your interpretation was and is accurate or inaccurate.

Appendix F

## Your 5 Important People in Your Life

Who are the 5 important people in your life? Who are the 5 important people who shaped the self concept that controls your life today, both positive and negative?

These are people who have played a unique and substantial role in creating the person you are today.

Now list the name of one pivotal person in your life. In two separate sections under that person's name, write first a description of the person's actions and then secondly, the influence that person has had on you.

Finally, were you on the list of the 5 important people in your life?

## Appendix G

## Personal Appreciation Inquiry: 4 Basics of Change
### (Identified by Cooperrider and Whitney)

1 **Discovery**—This is the stage in which people identify their best qualities, which have helped them the most in the past. The questions could range from "What am I best at?" to "What did I do previously that solved a similar situation?"

2 **Dream**—This is the stage in which people envision possibilities. The questions could include "What's the best thing that could come out of this problem?" or "Who can help me?"

3 **Design**—This is the stage in which people chart a course of action. The questions might be "Where's the best place to start?" or "How long will this take to succeed?"

4 **Delivery**—This is the action phase where the best questions might be "What's the first thing I need to do?" "What's next?" "What's the final step?"

To be happy, we must overcome fear, and the best way to overcome fear is with love. Many people cannot find their love. It exists, but it's buried beneath a cold snowdrift of hate. It's easy to hate. Hate does terrible interior damage. It tarnishes loves, hides love, and often kills love!

Appendix H

## 16 Best Personal Practices:
## Using Constructive Questions

1   What makes you happiest?

2   When were you happiest?

3   How did you become happy at that time?

4   What do you like most about yourself?

5   What creates that quality?

6   How do you make that quality last?

7   When did you have that quality the most?

8   How could you create more of it?

9   What gives you peace of mind?

10  What brings out the best in you?

11  Who appreciates you the most? Why?

12  What are your primary strengths?

13  What are your core beliefs?

14  What values do you live by?

15  Who is your emotional support network?

16   What best helps you feel creative?

The advantages of the above questions are helping people distinguish their strengths from their dreams. Dreams are good but too many people confuse what they wish they were good at with what they really are good at. They live in a dream world, idealistic world.

KC FOONG

# Appendix I

## 22 Ways to Power of Words

When deaf people talk to themselves in sign language, it activates the same area of the brain, the left interior frontal cortex, that is activated when hearing people talk to themselves. This area is adjacent to the brain's primary area of higher thought and because words make ideas real, engaging in self-talk enables all people, deaf or hearing, to make sense of their thoughts and gain access to their own wisdom.

Since self-talk is so powerful, it's important to choose your words carefully. If you use destructive language, you'll muddy your wisdom and create perceptions that can ruin your life. A good rule to follow in self-talk is to talk to yourself the way you want others to talk to you.

|  | CONSTRUCTIVE LANGUAGE | DESTRUCTIVE LANGUAGE |
|---|---|---|
| 1 | One possibility is... | You never... |
| 2 | It would be good to... | There's no way... |
| 3 | I love you when... | You should... |
| 4 | Thank you for... | I'm not good at... |
| 5 | I appreciate the... | What's the point of... |
| 6 | I like... | The problem with... |

| 7 | I understand why… | You don't understand… |
|---|---|---|
| 8 | Your best quality… | That's stupid… |
| 9 | People like you and me… | Don't go there… |
| 10 | The best part is… | It hurts to… |
| 11 | Have confidence… | He doesn't get it… |
| 12 | Please… | We'll lose if… |
| 13 | We'll succeed if we… | I'm better than… |
| 14 | It's okay to… | Listen to me… |
| 15 | My reasoning is… | Don't start… |
| 16 | I'm best at… | Would it kill to… |
| 17 | The good news is… | It's depressing when… |
| 18 | Let's make the best of… | When I was your age… |
| 19 | That's a good point… | I'm afraid that… |
| 20 | How can I help with… | This is the worst that… |
| 21 | It's my responsibility… | You make me… |

Appendix J

## Questions That Might Help Us
## Clarify Our Sense of Purpose

1   Am I living a life I love?

2   What brings vitality to my life?

3   What's my proudest achievement?

4   What does my life stand for?

5   What would I sacrifice my life for?

6   In what situation do I feel most alive?

7   What would I want on my tombstone?

## About the Author

KC Foong is a popular teacher, coach and mentor with a long successful career in both conventional classical and modern contemporary music performance and education in North America and Asia.

He is the founder of "Art of Piano Playing," Pianomagic KC," and has designed educational courses and syllabus for several Universities' Twinning Programs with their USA, UK and Australian partners where he also served as Examiner and Adjudicator.

Currently the President of Broadway Music Academy and Noah Life Coaching Center of Excellence, he works with individuals and groups to bring out the best from his students and guide them successfully through their professional lives, using his own unique abilities to spark interest, discover talents, and his strong and assuring motivation techniques.

KC Foong received his early education in the Methodist English School, Anglo Chinese School and the Methodist High School in Malaysia before pursuing his many passions in life in the USA, which includes the famous Kent State University in Kent, the Juilliard School in New York, Berklee College of Music in Boston, Trinity Evangelical Divinity School in Chicago and the Nassau Community College in Long Island where he took up "Drawing from the right side of the brain," "Karate," and "The Art of Magic for Fun."

KC has performed his favorite music in many parts of the world, been involved in mission trips and volunteering work. His original soundtracks have been broadcasted in 45 countries plus a solo piano CD, "Road to Your Heart," which was recorded and produced at the Reflections Studio in Los Angeles, California.

KC is available to speak and perform music around the globe. If you or your organization wishes to train personally with KC Foong, he can be reached at broadwaykc@gmail.com or www.kcfoong.com.

*"Living is a fine art,*
*like music or painting,*
*governed*
*by certain fundamental laws*
*that must be obeyed*
*to bring about the harmony, peace,*
*joy and happiness in life."*
ATTRIBUTION UNKNOWN

# Bibliography

Allison Dubois, WE ARE THEIR HEAVEN, Simon and Schuster Inc., New York 2006.

Audrey Ricker, HOW HAPPY FAMILIES HAPPEN, Hazelden 2006.

Ben Barry. FASHIONING REALITY, Key Porter Books Limited, Toronto 2007.

Barbara Sher, REFUSE TO CHOOSE! A REVOLUTIONARY PROGRAM FOR DOING EVERYTHING THAT YOU LOVE, Holtzbrinck Publishers, USA 2006.

Bill Bartman, BILLIONAIRE SECRETS TO SUCCESS, Brown Book Publishing 2005.

C. Norman Shealy, LIFE BEYOND 100: SECRETS OF THE FOUNTAIN OF YOUTH, Penguin Group, New York 2005.

Dan Baker, WHAT HAPPY PEOPLE KNOW: HOW THE SCIENCE OF HAPPINESS CAN CHANGE YOUR LIFE FOR THE BETTER, Rodale, USA 2003.

Dale Carnegie, HOW TO ENJOY YOUR LIFE AND YOUR JOB, Pocket Books, New York 1970, 1985.

Dale Carnegie, HOW TO STOP WORRYING AND START LIVING, Pocket Books, New York 1944, 1945, 1946, 1947, 1948, 1984.

Donald O. Clifton, NOW DISCOVER YOUR STRENGTH, Marcus Buckingham, the Free Press, New York 2001.

Donald Trump, THE WAY TO THE TOP, Crown Business, New York 2004.

Dave Lakhani, THE POWER OF AN HOUR, BUSINESS AND LIFE MASTERY IN ONE HOUR A WEEK, John Wiley & Sons, USA, Canada 2006.

Dean Barrett, SEARCH FOR THE PEACH BLOSSOM SPRING, Village East Books, USA 2004.

Daniel Drubin, LETTING GO OF YOUR BANANAS: HOW TO BECOME MORE SUCCESSFUL BY GETTING RID OF EVERYTHING ROTTEN IN YOUR LIFE, Warner Business Book, New York 2006.

Daniel Nettle, HAPPINESS: THE SCIENCE BEHIND YOUR SMILE, Oxford University Press 2006.

Daniel Gilbert, STUMBLING ON HAPPINESS, Alfred A. Knopp 2006.

Gary Small, 8 ESSENTIAL STRATEGIES FOR KEEPING YOUR MIND SHARP AND YOUR BODY YOUNG, Hyperion Books, New York 2006.

Hal Urban, CHOICES THAT CHANGE LIVES: 15 WAYS TO FIND MORE PURPOSE, MEANING AND JOY, Fireside, New York 2006.

Joel Osteen, DAILY READINGS FROM YOUR BEST LIFE NOW, Time Warner Book Group, New York 2005.

Joel Osteen, YOUR BEST LIFE NOW, Time Warner Book Group, New York 2004.

James Hollins, FINDING MEANING IN THE SECOND HALF OF YOUR LIFE: HOW TO FINALLY GROW UP, Penguin Group, New York 2005.

A SIMPLE GUIDE TO PERSONAL HAPPINESS

Joan Anderson, A WEEKEND TO CHANGE YOUR LIFE: FIND YOUR AUTHENTIC SELF AFTER A LIFETIME OF BEING ALL THINGS TO ALL PEOPLE, Broadway Books, New York 2006.

Joyce Meyer, IN PURSUIT OF PEACE, 21 WAYS TO CONQUER ANXIETY, FEAR AND DISCONTENTMENT, Time Warner Book Group, New York 2004.

Joanne Taylor, THERE YOU ARE, Tundra Books, Toronto, New York 2004.

Jonathon Haidt, THE HAPPINESS HYPOTHESIS, Basic Books 2005.

Keith Ablow, LIVING THE TRUTH, Hachette Book Group, New York 2007.

Larry Dossey, THE EXTRAORDINARY HEALING POWER OF ORDINARY THINGS: 14 NATURAL STEPS TO HEALTH AND HAPPINESS, Harmony Books, New York 2006.

Lillian Verner-Bonds, THE COMPLETE BOOK OF COLOR HEALING, PRACTICAL WAYS TO ENHANCE YOUR PHYSICAL AND SPIRITUAL WELL BEING, Sterling Publishing, New York 2000.

Matthew Ricard, A GUIDE TO DEVELOPING LIFE'S MOST IMPORTANT SKILLS: HAPPINESS, Little Brown Company, New York 2003.

Michael Adams, BETTER HAPPIER THAN RICH, CANADIANS, MONEY AND THE MEANING OF LIFE, Penguin Group, Toronto 2000.

Martin Seligman, AUTHENTIC HAPPINESS: USING THE NEW POSITIVE PSYCHOLOGY TO REALIZE YOUR POTENTIAL FOR LASTING FULFILLMENT, Free Press 2004.

Nicholas Perricone, 7 SECRETS TO BEAUTY, HEALTH AND LONGEVITY: THE MIRACLE OF CELLULAR REJUVENATION, Ballentine Books, New York 2006.

KC FOONG

Paul McKenna, CHANGE YOUR LIFE IN 7 DAYS, Harmony Books, Crown Publishing Group (Random House) New York 2004.

Patricia Lovett-Reid, LIVE WELL, RETIRE WELL, STRATEGIES FOR A RICH LIFE AND A RICHER RETIREMENT, TD Waterhouse, Canada 2006.

Philip McGraw, SELF MATTERS, Simon and Schuster Source, New York 2001.

Richard Branson, SCREW IT, LET'S DO IT: LESSONS IN LIFE, Virgin, London 2006.

Robert Kiyosaki, IF YOU WANT TO BE RICH AND HAPPY, DON'T GO TO SCHOOL, ENSURING LIFETIME SECURITY FOR YOURSELF AND YOUR CHILDREN, Asian Publishing, USA 1993.

Rick Warren, THE PURPOSE DRIVEN LIFE: WHAT ON EARTH AM I HERE FOR?, Zonderman, Michigan 2002.

Richard Carlson, EASIER THAN YOU THINK BECAUSE LIFE DOESN'T HAVE TO BE SO HARD, Harper Collins, New York 2005.

Robert Raines, A TIME TO LIVE: 7 TASKS OF CREATIVE AGING, Penguin Books 1997.

Robert Allen, MULTIPLE STREAMS OF INCOME: HOW TO GENERATE A LIFETIME OF UNLIMITED WEALTH! John Wiley & Sons, New Jersey, Canada, 2000, 2004.

Steve Biddulph, A PRACTICAL GUIDE TO HELPING MEN DISCOVER HEALTH, HAPPINESS AND DEEPER PERSONAL RELATIONSHIPS, Marlowe & company, New York, 1994, 1995, 2003.

Stephen M. Pollan and Mark Levine, IT'S ALL IN YOUR HEAD: THINKING YOUR WAY TO HAPPINESS: 8 ESSENTIAL SECRETS TO LEADING A LIFE WITHOUT REGRETS, Collins, New York 2006.

Sylvia Browne, LIGHT A CANDLE, Angel Bea Publishing, USA 2006.

Susan Newman, THE BOOK OF NO–250 WAYS TO SAY IT AND MEAN IT AND STOP PEOPLE PLEASING FOREVER, The McGraw-Hill companies, New York 2005.

Spencer Johnson, WHO MOVED MY CHEESE, G.P. PUTNAM & SON, 1998.

Wayne Dyer, INSPIRATION: YOUR ULTIMATE CALLING, Hay House, California 2006.

KC FOONG

ISBN 142513300-2

9 781425 133009